The complete guide to preparing and implementing service level agreements

About the first edition

'the book can be recommended . . . [It] is the first time the LIS profession has had a simple handbook on service level agreements . . . and practitioners will find much of assistance within its covers.'

Education for Information

'the whole process [of SLAs] is very professionally covered. Many of us will be grateful for this help and mentoring.'   *LA Record*

'this is the first book to offer information and library managers practical, step-by-step guidance to constructing and implementing an SLA.'   *Inform*

'Careful study of this work would allow most organizations to draw up a sensible and workable SLA. This book would easily pay for itself in avoiding expensive misunderstandings around service level agreements.'

Managing Information

The complete guide to preparing and implementing service level agreements

SECOND EDITION

Sheila Pantry OBE
Sheila Pantry Associates Ltd

Peter Griffiths
Head of Information Services Unit, Communication Directorate,
Home Office

LIBRARY ASSOCIATION PUBLISHING
LONDON

Published by
Library Association Publishing
7 Ridgmount Street
London WC1E 7AE

Library Association Publishing is wholly owned by The Library Association.

First published 1997
Second edition 2001

British Library Cataloguing in Publicaton Data

A catalogue record for this book is available from the British Library.

ISBN 1-85604-410-6

Typeset in 11/15pt Aldine 401 BT and Syntax by Library Association Publishing.
Printed and made in Great Britain by MPG Books Ltd, Bodmin, Cornwall.

CONTENTS

INTRODUCTION

This second edition shows that the LIS manager today continues to face many challenges in providing services that meet the requirements of all customers. In the public sector and the wider information marketplace the introduction of compulsory competitive tendering, market testing, value-for-money concepts, and more electronic services, coupled with downsizing and flatter management structure in organizations, have brought about significant changes. They have also had a profound impact on the way library and information services operate. Everyone in the LIS team is now conscious of the full implications of budgets, staff availability, and quality and level of service, and many are having to become adept at drawing up service level agreements.

Searching the literature has shown that there is still very little real guidance specifically aimed at the LIS practitioner about how to produce these complex and detailed documents. We hope that this book will help to close the gap in knowledge by providing useful ideas, hints, tips and phrases to be used when developing one. We have drawn on personal experience, and knowledge of cases where problems have arisen through lack of understanding between service provider and client.

In developing SLA courses and in writing the new edition of the book we have looked at and noted a wide range of documents not specifically belonging to the LIS sector, but which could be suitable for use in compiling an SLA. We urge readers to look at specific guidance that may exist in your own organizations, for example the Accountant's Department instructions in businesses and other organizations, and, for government LIS readers, HM Treasury publications. We have included such titles in the reading lists to enlarge the reader's own knowledge and we acknowledge these documents and authors.

Each chapter is written to help you through the various stages of establishing your own service level agreements with your clients and with your suppliers. Chapter 1 gives you the origins and use of SLAs; Chapter 2 describes an SLA and its main features, while Chapter 3 tells you who the agreement is between and which items you need to consider for inclusion. Chapter 4 describes what an SLA should look like and supplies descriptions of services that can be included in the SLA, while Chapters 5 and 6 give information on service monitoring and charging for services. Managing customers, outsourcing, managing suppliers and e-suppliers are discussed in Chapters 7, 8, 9 and 10. It is important to keep LIS staff informed of the developments and communication strategies needed in producing the SLA and these are discussed in Chapters 11 and 12. The various appendices will give you even more help by the inclusion of: further possible items to be added to an SLA; further reading; and a sample SLA.

Once you have an SLA we urge you to keep checking and revising it to ensure that all the detail is correct and up to date and that you do not leave yourself vulnerable. Jobs and tasks change and so must the SLA!

Your SLA will help show how successful you are in providing the services needed. The very act of developing the agreement and focusing in detail on each separate service element has spin-off benefits enabling you to focus on important issues such as the following:

- Why are we providing this service?
- Should it be continued?
- Is there a better way?
- What should be provided?
- Is it really needed in the format provided?
- When is it done? Why then – can a better time be found?
- Where is it done? Why there – can a better place be found?
- Can someone else provide it?

Library and information services are vital to the well-being of organizations however small or large, whether in the private or public sector. By providing quality and appropriate services your information service should succeed.

We wish you every success.

Peter Griffiths writes in a personal capacity but is grateful for the Home Office's agreement to publish his contribution to this book. Nothing in this text should be taken as a description of official practice, and mention of any commercial service or product does not imply any official endorsement.

Sheila Pantry and Peter Griffiths

1

THE ORIGINS AND USE OF SERVICE LEVEL AGREEMENTS

In this chapter we examine:

- the nature and origin of service level agreements (SLAs)
- legislative and other drivers for their adoption
- why they are used in library and information services (LIS)
- particular issues arising from their use in LIS
- general principles for the compilation of SLAs.

The developing role of the SLA

At the time when we produced the first edition of this book, the service level agreement (SLA) was being used in a number of specialized situations in the library and information services arena. Often, it followed an unnerving experience such as the hiving-off of a service or the decision to set it on a commercial footing, and was used to regulate the relationship between the central organization and the outsourced section.

Now SLAs are in far more general use. Many people are familiar with them through the arrangements they have with internet service providers (ISPs), and many of us in the profession routinely work with them to manage or deliver library and information services. Although new issues have emerged since the original edition of this book, it has become clearer that SLAs are not of themselves a bad thing, and that with a sensible approach on both sides they can form a foundation for the development of improved services.

The nature and definition of SLAs

The service level agreement (SLA) has much in common with a contract, with which it is often confused. But it has some essential differences that make it particularly suited to use in certain circumstances, as we will show shortly.

The SLA has been defined as a 'proxy contract', that is, a formal agreement between two parties to a service, which, however, has no legal effect. It represents the goodwill and faith of the parties signing it, but the parties will not – and frequently cannot – sue each other if it does not work out. So the SLA does not have the watertight nature of a contract, and problems of failure can be particularly difficult to resolve.

It is always a challenge to encapsulate the nature of a complex document in a few words to be read by someone who is unfamiliar with its nature. You will find a number of definitions of service level agreements if you search the literature listed in the reading list to this volume, or indeed if you read the flyers for various courses that may fall on to your desk. By examining some of these definitions, we can identify the essential elements of these documents.

One definition is that an SLA is 'a statement of available service levels from which the client or customer will select one level specifying timing, frequency, etc.'[1] Another is that the SLA is 'an agreement between the provider of a service and its customers which quantifies the minimum quantity of service which meets the business need'.[2]

A more useful definition is that the SLA is 'a negotiated agreement, agreed between the parties, which quantifies the minimum level of service and sets out costs and criteria for delivery'.[3] This contains the essence of the agreement in four statements.

First, the SLA is a negotiated agreement. The customer(s) have set out their requirements, and in return the supplier has said what is on offer. This in itself is a fundamental change for many organizations: as we will show again and again in this book, traditionally, the provider has stated what is available and the customer has been encouraged to accept it. For perhaps the first time SLAs ask the customer to state a requirement, which the supplier – the LIS in this case – is to meet.

There will probably be further bargaining and negotiating on levels or costs before the next stage: the parties have agreed on a common level, which they are both prepared to sign up to, taking into account their costs and resources, and so on.

It follows that this agreement is for a minimum level of service. It does not preclude there being different levels of service (and costs) for different customers, nor does it preclude there being different levels for different services to the same customer. As we will show later in this book, an SLA is very likely to contain exactly these variations as the customer juggles resources against the needs of various groups within the organization.

But there will be a statement of what the supplier is going to supply (or what can be supplied if necessary) and what the customer agrees to accept from that range of offers. Many suppliers find the simplest thing to do is to include their standard documentation and brochure prospectuses in the agreement and to use an annex as a schedule of items for delivery. There will probably be a further statement specifying what happens if the supply is not delivered.

Finally there is likely to be a schedule of costs and resource requirements. This again goes closely with the statement of criteria for the service.

The two earlier definitions are useful as a gloss on this statement. The first points out that there is choice from a range of options, although it is rather short on showing that the SLA is an agreement as well as a statement. The second one usefully draws attention to the concept of business need, although it could have said whose. In fact, the customer's business need – for information in this case – will be matched against the supplier's business need to contain costs within available resources while retaining the business.

Three objectives can therefore be identified in an SLA. First, it identifies and states customer need, in the form of a service statement, which either stands in its own right or else is modified as a statement of customer need by a schedule stating which services are selected from a larger list.

Second, it analyses the processes of fulfilling that need. This takes the form of statements of *what* is to be done, not necessarily saying *how* it will be done, unless the closely defined performance of routine is critical to the operation. This is where statements of frequency or scope can be useful. For example, in order to meet a customer need for up-to-date marketing information, an information service might provide a current awareness bulletin, which the SLA would state was to appear every Friday by 12 noon. But it would be unhelpful to include a list of the journals scanned in the SLA because it would require change control to be invoked every time a new journal was added, or if someone saw a relevant article in another journal not on the list. This second objective, the analysis of fulfilment of the need, also provides the supplier's statement of need, and answers the first objective.

Third, the SLA records the means of measuring performance in carrying out these processes and may define levels of activity. The agreement of both parties and the relationship to the business needs of each is thus registered.

SLAs in the public sector

The use of SLAs has been particularly common in the public sector, although their origin is in the management of large internal suppliers (such as computer centres) within private and educational organizations. Central and local government have been greatly fragmented in recent years, with the result that two kinds of relationship now occur in SLAs, interdepartmental and intradepartmental.

The first relationship is closely akin to a contract. The parties may be government departments, they may be local authorities, or they may be executive agencies, direct labour or supply organizations, or other public bodies. The use of the interdepartmental SLA is to overcome the fact that an organization cannot sue itself. Government departments and agencies all form part of the Crown, which is indivisible in law. Similarly, a local authority and its direct supply organization may well be organized so that they are not separate legal entities and cannot have recourse to law to settle disputes.

The second use, to regulate intradepartmental activity, occurs where a section or division of an organization operates as a mini-business within the parent, and regulates its relationship with an SLA. This is common after compulsory tenders have been won by an in-house team, and is found in a number of areas including libraries, records management, computer services and other information-related activities.

The development of SLAs in the UK public sector

There are three major areas of the UK public sector where SLAs are found: local government, the National Health Service and central government. There is also a fourth group comprising other services.

Local government

Local government reforms in the early 1980s paved the way for the use of SLAs. The Local Government, Planning and Land Act 1980[4] put highways and building construction and maintenance work out to tender. A second measure, the Local Government Act 1988,[5] extended compulsory competitive tendering (CCT) to a wider range of services: refuse collection, the cleaning of buildings, street cleaning, catering, ground maintenance, the repair and maintenance of vehicles, and (perhaps most relevant given the organization of some local authority leisure services), the management of sports and leisure facilities. This was the first occasion on which CCT had been brought into a professional area.

More recently, local government and other areas of the public service have been concerned with the concept of 'best value', which was introduced through the White Paper *Modern local government in touch with the people*.[6] This, and other parallel strands such as the work arising from *Reading the future*,[7] has focused attention on new ways of defining and measuring library services within the context of service level management. Later in this chapter we will look at one example of the new ideas that have emerged.

National Health Service (NHS)

The NHS Management Enquiry,[8] otherwise known as the 'Griffiths report' after its chairman Sir Roy Griffiths, led to a profound change in culture, replacing the old consensus style of management with a new system of management accountability. By the time the *Working for Patients* White Paper[9] was published in 1989, the philosophy was well developed and definitions had evolved. In terms of this survey, the main feature was the development of a division of

5

healthcare into two elements, the purchaser (the health authority, or later fund-holder general practitioners (GPs)) and the provider (primarily, the hospitals). In particular, by devolving money from the health authorities to the GPs, the health departments took a highly significant step from the SLA viewpoint: they put qualified and competent healthcare professionals involved in service delivery into the purchaser group, creating a cadre of intelligent customers who were able to define in terms of their own professional expertise the service that they required from their suppliers. In practice there has been criticism that it is still the providers – mainly the hospitals – who have had the major role in defining services they will offer to the purchasers.

Central government

Central government has seen a similar range of initiatives[10] since the early 1980s. The Rayner Scrutinies[11] in the early 1980s aimed to identify ways in which departmental activities could be carried out more efficiently, and some early reviews of government libraries took place under these scrutinies. The *Financial Management Initiative*[12] followed in which departments were asked to look at their management systems and financial procedures in order to improve accountability for and the use of resources. Importance was attached to techniques such as the development of performance measures, although the benefit of some of this work would probably have been increased had some departmental rules been relaxed to allow greater freedom to managers.

In 1988 came the 'Efficiency Unit report'[13] known variously as the 'Ibbs report' (after its author) and lately as the 'Next steps report' (after its subtitle). In this scheme, the executive function of departments was to be separated from policy-making, and the executive arm, which was often the interface with the public, was to become a separate agency with defined tasks in support of a defined role expressed in a framework document. This document would set out objectives and performance levels – to all intents and purposes it would be a form of SLA. In these documents, the purpose of the agency is described, its relationship to the parent department, its functions, the tasks to be performed in support of the functions, and the levels at which they should be performed. Some also contain a section setting out the services to be provided by one partner to the other, recognizing the difficulty of making a total separation of department and agency from the outset, which is a feature that can usefully be part of any LIS SLA.

The 'next steps' concept has altered considerably since the first edition of this book. There is no longer a next steps team in the Cabinet Office and the annual report now refers simply to 'agencies'. The number of agencies has fallen by a quarter, but there have been movements and amalgamations. One of the highest profile changes has been the merger of the Contributions Agency (Department of Social Security) into the Inland Revenue, which has allowed a more integrated approach.[14]

The Private Finance Initiative concept, introduced in the early 1990s to introduce private sector funding and shared risk to major public sector projects, has extended and evolved in central government. Perhaps surprisingly, a major development in the use of PFI funding for libraries has been in its extension to the design and construction of library buildings. Brighton and Hove Council, for example, was reported early in 2001 to be setting design quality as the prime criterion in evaluating PFI tenders for its own new library building. A related innovation in this field is the development of the Public Private Partnership (PPP) and the PPP Programme (or PPPP). As might be anticipated from the name, the PPPP brings together public and private sector partners to develop major projects; while these are likely to be larger-scale developments than a branch library, there is scope for the use of PPPP in big projects. The service level management approach has strong appeal in terms of helping to define the deliverables of such projects.

Competing for quality[15] is the White Paper that produced the concept of market testing that was widely used in the early 1990s, and it is still present in some of the tests of the best value process. However the paper has little to say on SLAs apart from a comment that they should replicate as far as possible the disciplines of a contractual relationship. In particular, managers should audit the performance of an in-house operation as rigorously as an external contract, in order to ensure that efficiency gains are delivered.

Other public service examples of SLAs

Other areas of the public sector also make use of SLAs. Some police forces use SLAs to set out internal agreements on services. Thames Valley Police operates its Complaints and Discipline Department in this way, setting out performance standards and including terms that the Unit wishes its customers to apply.[16] (We will show in a later chapter that it is essential to obtain customers' agreement to some terms and obligations under an SLA.)

The Prison Service does not operate its own libraries in prison establishments in England and Wales, but enters into an SLA with the local authority to provide a service at each prison. A publication issued by the Prison Service[17] included a skeleton SLA which is adaptable enough to be used whether a local authority treats a prison library as being a fully fledged branch library, or akin to a form of housebound readers' service. The model is also notable for incorporating reference to other documents, such as a governor's contract and a prisoners' compact, as forming a part of the SLA.

The effects of using SLAs

The introduction of SLAs obviously has a profound effect on the organization. Old management lines are broken and a formal contract is introduced at some point in a previously continuous chain to manage a service. Sometimes the senior manager of the new service is at a lower level than before, with the previous service manager now taking charge of contract management. The contracted-in management structure may well be flatter than its predecessor. It may be that the new contract manager knows little or nothing of the previous culture of the service, or that the transfer of a senior officer to contract management robs the new service of its most experienced managers and mentors. Informal but effective working methods may be lost if sufficient care is not taken with the SLA and the manner of performing tasks is specified rather than the outcomes.

Care is also needed to ensure that contract management of the SLA in the restructured organization does not take place within the same direct management line as the operation of the contract. It is clearly invidious for the service manager to report to the contract manager. Not only does this make it difficult to separate the operational management issues from the personnel issues, but the conflict of interests makes this a weak link in the management chain. The organization's interests may be best served by supporting a LIS when, for example, service delivery has been affected by failure of a supplier. But where the contract manager is also the line manager he or she may concentrate more on considering the LIS manager's standard of performance in allowing the situation to arise.

Innovative good practice through SLAs

Since the first edition of this book, a number of innovative library service schemes have drawn directly or indirectly on the SLA principle to develop new schemes that set a level of best practice that other providers could draw upon. In particular, a number of the proposals contained in *Reading the future* have been developed, with varying levels of success.

It is now common for libraries to outsource a number of activities. Here, we look at the types of library services that have been outsourced successfully or otherwise, while in Chapter 8 we look in more detail at the considerations that you will need to take into account when setting up outsourcing arrangements.

Some activities such as book jacketing have of course been carried out by book suppliers for many years, but service level agreement techniques allow a better definition, and thus better understanding between the library and the supplier. Other activities have followed: there are for example several reports of security tagging and other servicing tasks also being outsourced within service level agreements.

Liverpool's libraries have taken the more radical step of placing book selection into the hands of the book supplier.[18] Library staff worked with the book suppliers to produce detailed specifications of requirements, with commitment being ensured by involving all those currently doing the work in the specifications process – an important piece of good practice. Among the issues highlighted in the reports of this experiment is the need to include guidelines on the proportion of hardbacks and paperbacks to be supplied (something that the Library and Information Statistics Unit at Loughborough University had also drawn attention to). Remarkable too is the fact that the specification had gone through 17 editions by the time it was reported; but as we will show later, the specification and other papers are living documents and need to be updated whenever necessary.

A more far-reaching approach has been the creation of library trusts, again following a recommendation contained in *Reading the future*. A feasibility study in Dorset during 1994 looked at the potential in the provision of library services for the use of trusts – that is, the transfer of the service to a charitable limited company that would then provide a specified level of service under contract to the local authority. The survey concluded that this would be both feasible and beneficial, since when the most notable example has been the London Borough of Hounslow. Community Initiative Partnerships[19] is a charitable trust that took responsibility for leisure service provision in Hounslow (including the libraries) in 1998, under an agreement with Hounslow Council.

Other forms of partnership have included CD-ROM loan services provided through commercial partnership (such as Ramesis, now part of Chivers), IT training (Input Output Centres in various libraries, mainly in London, or Connect To Libraries learning centres on Merseyside).

Service specification is an important element of any such activity, and increasingly the framework documents that create these services are available on the world wide web.

We look further at these issues in the context of outsourcing in Chapter 8.

The SLA goes full circle

We noted earlier that SLAs had come to library and information services from their origins in information technology services. Now, they are increasingly being encountered as a means of managing internet services and connections. Internet service providers (ISPs) are reluctant to guarantee service levels in absolute terms because of the potential of the ensuing payments for service failure to cripple their businesses, even if the underlying failure was not of their making. As a result they express service availability levels as an agreement and not as a contract. Libraries and information services making use of the internet either to search for or to publish information will encounter SLAs in both contexts. Similarly, the use of service level agreements to regulate dealings with application service providers (ASPs), who effectively rent the use of software over the internet, has developed for the same reasons. We now see that the use of SLAs has gone full circle, and is being used once more to regulate IT services, but this time between the organization and a third party in order to avoid the penalties of a formal contract.

Their use has not been entirely successful to date, in two respects. One issue is that the problems of measurement and monitoring, which we consider in Chapter 5, have been given too little consideration by organizations agreeing the terms of the documents put before them. Poorly constructed documents disguise the fact that a service level below around 99.7% is of little use to a serious internet publisher, since at this level of downtime entire days of connection can be lost. This effect can be compounded if the agreement does not also specify a maximum duration of each single service loss, perhaps limiting it to four hours before penalties are invoked and problem escalation occurs.

A survey carried out in early 2001 by a network-monitoring software company suggested that over 80% of UK ISPs were breaching their agreements in any month. Users were owed additional time in compensation worth £30 million as a result, and could expect a total loss of service time amounting to two million hours in a year. However, because many users do not actively monitor the service available to them, they were unaware of the time owing to them.[20]

Thinking the unthinkable

Before we go on to look at specific aspects of service level agreements, here is a final further collection of general issues to bear in mind.

The SLA compiler needs to think the unthinkable, and to consider every reasonable possibility that might arise. Is weekend overtime working to be included, and in what circumstances? (Does the LIS have any role to play in emergency procedures, for example, be it to provide information, lend staff, or offer its premises? If there were a public health crisis or epidemic, what would the LIS do?) General phrases such as 'by agreement' avoid the need to spell out a list of possible disaster scenarios, but a time of need is not the time to discover that a change control meeting is needed.

The SLA is often considered restrictive,[21] but need not be so in practice. New models of service delivery can be established alongside SLAs and can operate in parallel if need be. These parallel activities could include new partnership arrangements to deliver innovative services, or could mean the traditional funding of services that are excluded from the SLA until renegotiation allows them to be added to the new version. SLAs cannot, on the other hand, do anything to alter restrictive accounting procedures in the customer organization, or to alter the customer's house style on telephone answering, or the wearing of name badges and even uniforms for some members of LIS staff.

SLAs are as much an innovation for suppliers as for customers. They are not intended to provide suppliers with training in service level management at the customer's expense. Suppliers may need persuading that to share their management information with the customer will help both sides to manage the contract, and perhaps to prevent small problems becoming major conflicts that threaten the contract. Where the supplier is in a one-to-one-only position with the customer (typically the in-house supplier), there is no scope to develop solutions that can be shared among a group of customers, or to benefit from diversification into another market. Technology transfer is difficult where there is only one customer and one supplier in the market.

Summary

This chapter has set the scene for what follows by explaining the uses of service level agreements in LIS and showing some examples of the situations in which they are encountered. It has also set out some of the considerations in moving to service level management, and indicated areas of concern in setting up management systems involving SLAs.

Points on which to reflect

- What questions are important in your organization in working on service level management?
- What information exists about service standards and provision on which an SLA could be based?
- How could service level agreements help in managing service innovations in your library?
- Are you expected to agree the terms of other people's service level agreements without the opportunity to influence the conditions that are included?

2

WHAT IS A SERVICE LEVEL AGREEMENT?

In this chapter you will find details on the following:

- **what an SLA is**
- **why an SLA is important to you**
- **an outline of an SLA**
- **the features of an SLA**
- **what should be put in an annex**
- **why there is a need to use tight definitions**
- **the issues concerning negotiations.**

Introduction

In recent years, SLAs have become a common part of LIS activities. The debate continues as to whether an SLA will get in the way of providing a good service or enable the LIS to have more control on the types and levels of services provision. Looking at the more positive side, a number of benefits can be derived from having an SLA: all parties to the agreement, including the users, will have a better understanding of the services available, the quality of the services and the modes of delivery.

Why do we need SLAs?

As you saw in the previous chapter, SLAs have no legal effect, but it is important to set out clearly the relationships between the suppliers of the service(s) and the users. Both sides need a benchmark, against which to test the efficiency and effectiveness of the services and products provided. The service provider must know the standards to which they must conform. Ultimately, any service can be measured against these standards, and, if the service is found to be unsatisfactory, the SLA can be withdrawn and the functions re-tendered.

The supplier of the service and the user will each be accountable for what they do, or don't do. So it is essential for each party to have a clear understanding of their respective roles and responsibilities so that neither party has any doubts about the extent to which they are accountable.

In an SLA, suppliers and users of services are clearly identified and develop an understanding of each other's requirements and abilities. Suppliers are clearly accountable for the performance standards, quality and cost of their services, and any limitations or shortcomings.

On the other hand, users should clearly understand the cost of such services, and of any additional ones that may be required either within the existing agreement or in addition to it. The agreement should be such that users can monitor the volume and quality of services they are paying for, and the suppliers can monitor their own capabilities and, if necessary, improve, by training, the staff offering the services. And at all times, both suppliers and users should understand the mechanism for variation or termination of services.

What is an SLA?

First, what exactly is the nature of an SLA? We saw it described earlier as a proxy contract – one which takes the place of a formal contract. But it is a contract, in that it is an agreement, usually between two parties, detailing the essential elements of services with timescales and performance levels to be provided by the supplier to the client. So to that extent it is binding and represents the goodwill of the parties, who have agreed on a level of services to which both (or all) can sign up, taking financial, staffing and other resources into account. Whether or not there are varying service levels for separate parts of the customer organization, the SLA says what the supplier is going to supply and what the customer agrees to accept in that supply. The SLA should set out the way in which the service is going to be delivered, and what happens if it isn't. The LIS may choose to put this information into a statement of service or standard brochure or guide, and then first refer to it in the agreement. It is entirely up to the supplier and the customer to agree on this.

Whichever course is chosen by the LIS, however, it is a useful exercise to have prepared a list of the services that it provides, including definitions as necessary. Even within LIS there is considerable confusion over the multiple meanings of words such as 'circulation', 'series' and 'copy':[1] distinctions may well be lost by management staff putting together an operational requirement without the benefit of professional advice. These contract managers may well rely on trade literature to guide their efforts: this literature is frequently of American origin and uses American terminology such as 'routing' and the American sense of terms such as 'circulation'. If you mean journal circulation say so; if you mean book circulation in the sense of the old-fashioned circulating library, say that. A moment's reflection will show that the document in question moves quite differently in each case, and its transits to and from the LIS are far greater in the second instance than the first. If it is necessary to draw out a distinction between 'circulation' (where the items circulated return to the LIS) and 'distribution' (where the users retain the documents sent to them), then draw that distinction in your glossary. Precision in such matters at the outset will save considerable problems during the performance of the SLA.

Basic objectives of the SLA

The SLA has the following basic objectives:

- It states what the customer needs by providing a service statement.
- It shows the mechanics and processes of fulfilling those needs.
- It describes the volumes to be handled and the ways of measuring them.

In doing this the SLA records the following pieces of information:

- What the purchaser wishes to buy and therefore what the supplier is expected to provide.
- The nature of the agreed services, in such a way that it is precise enough to act as an agreement but not so prescriptive that it prevents service development or precludes negotiated change to improve service.

Why an SLA is important

In an SLA, it is essential that all levels of staff are involved in the compilation of the agreement, because everyone's personal performance, understanding of the levels of services to be achieved and the timescales within which these levels of services are to be given are implicit in the agreement. Job descriptions and the required levels of performance will be derived from the SLA through the business planning process, and the time to discover that there are problems is not during the job appraisal exercise a year later.

Therefore, at whatever level you are working you need to be aware of the full implications of an SLA, often because it is the person working at, for example, the enquiry desk, the interlibrary loans section, the search service section, or the ordering section, who has the most detailed knowledge of the systems that will have to meet any agreements. For instance it is no good agreeing to providing an interlibrary loans service on terms stating that an item can usually be delivered within 48 hours when you know the norm is more like four days.

Features of an SLA

SLAs were first widely used to manage relations with corporate computing sections and have a number of features that reflect their origins. They are often a feature of quality management systems where their precision aids the process of definition of products and services. They clarify the relationship

17

between the supplier and the customer by setting out expectations and responsibilities, and the commitment of both parties to the agreement. Setting out the customer's responsibilities in the contract as well as the supplier's should avoid any unnecessary arguments, for example where the customer has more details about a requested document than they actually reveal. Most information workers will have experienced the situation where a customer asks vaguely for some reference only to find that they have all the details in front of them but omitted to tell the information section! The implied suggestion is that it is up to the supplier to find the item required with no further clues. And the SLA is a planning tool for the supplier, by allowing the prediction of troughs and peaks of activity.

The SLA is prescriptive, but this should be of what is to be done rather than how. To describe and define the required result is useful; to say how it is to be achieved is unnecessarily restrictive. There are often alternative and possibly better ways of achieving the end, which the supplier may be freer to implement than was the management line.

The SLA should include details of exceptions to the agreement, particularly anticipated and permissible exceptions. If a standard service is provided (which we saw may be defined in a brochure or service statement) then the agreement need only refer to the standard terms and then list the variations, exceptions or enhancements.

The SLA will contain elements of a number of different types of specification in a single document. These include:

- *Functional specification*: a definition of what the system has to achieve or do, probably expressed in terms of outputs or achievements.
- *Performance specification*: setting levels of performance, for example by setting a minimum quota of actions to be completed in a stated time for various LIS functions ('90% of enquiries from the management floor to be answered within 60 minutes').
- *Technical specification*: although it is to be avoided so far as possible, in practical terms it is probably not possible in many LIS to exclude a definition of some of the systems and services to be used ('The LIS will use

the XYZ Ltd connection to Internet Services Providers Ltd for external electronic mail communications').

What SLAs do not do

SLAs need not be restrictive, although they can be and have been in practice
when too little imagination is used and the agreed terms allow no freedom
to develop.

New models of service delivery can be established alongside the SLA:
they have often proved to be necessary to fill in areas missed in the service definition, and partnerships have been set up with external suppliers to develop
additional services or to provide investment in new areas. However the SLA
still seems to fit better with the supplier used to the public sector working style.

SLAs still hit problems when faced with something as impenetrable as government accounting systems and Treasury rules. Companies might well be
content with systems of accountability that are less rigid, but it will not be
possible at present for in-house suppliers in many public sector organizations
to include alternative systems in the proposal and SLA.

Other things SLAs do not do

SLAs are a new way of working for suppliers of services. They are not a form
of training and in-house teams need to be signed up to them in advance. They
don't improve management accounting, particularly if they don't call on both
sides to share information that they may gather either as part of performance
monitoring or in order to manage the service.

This is particularly difficult in the public service where there has tended
to be a one-supplier, one-consumer system for most contracts. In the private
sector a company will typically have a number of clients, and will develop
products or services in line with the wishes of some of those clients before
offering the new product to its other customers. In the public sector, the in-
house supplier has no other clients with whom to develop new services or
to create new markets.

Negotiating and signing the SLA

General considerations

The actual negotiation and signing of the SLA also raises a number of issues. These issues are clarified first by looking at the client and supplier roles. In LIS the signatory as supplier will be the head of the LIS, and the signatory as client might be as follows:

- *in a public library*: the manager of the department of leisure activities and public libraries
- *in a government library*: the principal establishment officer or a director at management board level
- *in a special library*: the manager of corporate services or other senior manager
- *in an academic library*: the chair or secretary of the academic council.

It is important to ensure that the signatory on behalf of the customer is not either at a higher level in the same management chain as the LIS manager, or the same signatory as for the client side; otherwise resolution of any problems will be extremely difficult.

In the first instance, it is undesirable for performance appraisal that the reporting of the LIS manager as an individual be bound up with reporting systems that monitor the performance of the contract. It is quite possible for the LIS manager to perform at a high level of skill and efficiency while at the same time the contract governed by the SLA is failing. There should be clear separation of the two issues, although in practice it may be difficult to achieve total separation in a small organization or where there is a narrow management structure. It may be necessary to provide suitable training for procurement staff in order to allow them to report on contract performance in other business commands within the organization.

In the second instance, the same senior person is signatory for both sides, or is the manager for both the supplier and the client managers, there will be problems in case of dispute: the senior manager will in effect be arguing with him or herself. It may be necessary to dissuade board members from placing themselves in this difficult position through excessive desire to be involved in SLA management. The ideal is for any dispute to be settled at a lower level, leaving the most senior manager available in case of appeal or to provide final settlement of an evenly balanced argument.

Considering these possibilities also highlights the problems of negotiation. Particularly where there is an element of competition, such as in a compulsory competitive tender, the LIS management chain, as a potential supplier, must be excluded from the team defining the service requirement. This is likely to cause problems in reaching an accurate specification. The client side team needs to have a full description of LIS services available from the outset of its work, so it is helpful for an LIS that is likely to be faced with CCT to have published a fully defined service statement well in advance of the competition. Otherwise it would be reasonable to insist that the client side engages a consultant with LIS experience who is, preferably, acceptable to both client and supplier teams.

Agreement strategies

The service level agreement may be for only a part of the service, especially where a tendering process has been used. For example, in some contracts the value-added services (enquiries, selective dissemination of information (SDI), loans, online services) have been awarded to the existing LIS under service level agreement, while publications supply is outsourced. A similar approach has developed where direct purchasing organizations have been set up for local authority and other LIS services.

In this case the SLA with the LIS should state clearly which services are to be provided under the agreement, and the LIS should use the opportunity to define any conditions relating to a third party's services. For example, the LIS may wish to include a statement measuring delivery times exclusive of the time taken by the publications supplier (bookseller or serials agent) to obtain a publication, or the time taken by the internal mail service to collect an urgent item from the LIS and deliver it to the user.

There is also a need for specific statements where the LIS uses, or wishes to use, external contractors for parts of its work (such as indexing, or updating looseleaf publications). Alternatively, if the client has adopted the policy of offering several different packages for tender and agreement, the LIS may be faced with using external services for the first time in what it had previously considered an integral part of its service. In either case, this will be considered as subcontracting in some situations and needs to be carefully specified where this is part of the strategy adopted by either party to the agreement.

The agreement will clearly need to specify some other details such as the starting date, conditions for payment where this applies, and any conditions concerning equipment or other services that must be used by the supplier. (This might, for example, prevent the LIS from changing to another computer system considered to be better than the existing one, or able to use electronic data interchange with a supplier.)

Multiple agreements

A variation on the offer of a part of the service for agreement is the offer of multiple agreements. This situation may arise through the gradual introduction of SLAs in a large organization, with the LIS setting up agreements initially with small departments and maybe arriving at an umbrella agreement for the whole organization at a later date.

Great care is needed to keep these agreements in line. In a busy LIS it is impossible to prioritize clients into those entitled to a two-day service and those entitled to a one-day service for the same request. In practice it is likely to be difficult enough to keep track of senior management requests being processed separately. If an organization-wide SLA is introduced the LIS manager should request either that the terms of all SLAs are identical, or preferably that the existing SLAs should be cancelled and replaced by the new one. This avoids the possibility of later changes to the original SLAs bringing back differential qualities of service, and the need to maintain multiple agreements, thus adding to the load of the LIS's contract managers. (This is not of course to preclude the offer of a premium service to those clients prepared to pay more than the normal subscription under the blanket SLA.) The

Audit Commission argues convincingly for this approach in its second volume of advice on managment of central services under contracts and agreements.[2]

Agreement monitoring

Chapter 5 is devoted to service monitoring, and the detailed mechanisms are explored there. But it is important at the agreement drafting stage to ensure that monitoring systems are built in; that both sides are committed to them not as an inconvenience but as a basis for discussion and understanding between the two sides. At the early stages of working with SLAs, it must be a function of the senior management of LIS to gain staff commitment to their constructive use, and to build monitoring procedures into the quality management strategy of the organization.

Conclusion

In these opening chapters we have looked at the general principles of working with SLAs and indicated the approach to be taken to developing and implementing them in the LIS sector. In the following part of this book we show the outline of a typical SLA. Chapters 3 and 4 will give you more of the details, while Chapters 5 and 6 will give you details of costs and monitoring the SLA. Chapters 7 and 8 will show you how to manage both your suppliers and your customers. We do not guarantee a magic prescription in these chapters, but at least you have been forewarned!

Summary

An ideal SLA should comprise a short covering contract document, to which is appended a detailed specification with annexes containing other details and amendments.

The essential elements of a covering contract document include the following:

- A brief general statement summarizing the services to be provided (full details are in the specification or even the brochure or guide).
- Definitions of the two parties to the agreement – who is providing the service (supplier) to whom (client).
- A statement of the duration of the contract.
- Other important specific information such as dependencies on related agreements.

3

Who the agreement is between and the other items you need to put into the SLA

In this chapter you will find details on the following:

- definitions to be used
- who the agreement is between
- the period of time the agreement should cover
- what other items you need to include
- services
- value-added tax (VAT)
- resolution of disputes and default
- duty of care and hours of work
- premises and facilities
- variations of requirements and amendments to the agreement
- monitoring, costs and responsibilities.

Who the agreement is between and the definitions to be used

Perhaps the most important aspect of the SLA is defining exactly who the agreement is between and what constitutes the main clauses. You will also need to spell out the general conditions of the SLA; perhaps this information is best relegated to an annexe. You will need particularly to define the words and phrases used.

As we mentioned earlier, even commonly used words and phrases in LIS can have different meanings to the supplier and the customer, and some are ambiguous between the in-house supplier and external companies. As you devise and amend the SLA, you will need to ensure that any new terms used are defined and agreed by the parties concerned.

The sections set in **sans serif font** throughout the text show typical paragraphs and definitions of terms that can be used as contract statements in SLAs. They are intended to help you in defining your own list of words and phrases and also to indicate some of the various paragraphs that should be included in your SLA. A number of these have been adapted for specific use by LIS from standard terms and conditions for public sector contracts.

General preamble

You need to include some general terms and statements at the beginning of the SLA, in the manner of a contract. This is to avoid the need for repetition, and to clarify common problems in setting out agreements. Note that, apart from the definition of what is meant by the LIS, we are not yet defining anything that could be said to be specifically about services.

In the following document:

'The customer' means the receiver of the service ['The Department Manager'];

'XYZ LIS' means the library and information services section of XYZ organization and is the provider of the services ['The Agreement Holder'];

'The Agreement' means the agreement concluded between the customer and XYZ organization's LIS, including this document, all specifications, plans and other documents that are relevant to it. In case of discrepancy among these documents, this document (as amended by any subsequent annexes and schedules) prevails;

'Department' means a department in the organization if the term is not otherwise qualified by its context;

'The Agreed Budget' means the budget allocated to the LIS for the full and proper performance by the LIS of their part of the Agreement as determined under the provisions of the Agreement;

'Sub-contractor' means any person, firm or company under contract to the organization to perform work or provide professional services and/or supply goods in connection with the agreement and includes any other person or persons taken as a partner or director by such person, firm or company during the currency of the Agreement and the surviving member or members of any such firm or company;

'The premises' means the premises described in the specification;

'The specification' means the description and specification in the first part of this document;

The masculine includes the feminine;

The singular includes the plural and vice versa;

'Month' means calendar month unless otherwise defined.

Services

Now you will need to decide what services are being agreed subject to the provision of the agreement. We suggest some wording such as:

to provide services, as listed in the Schedule (Annexe C to the Agreement), and defined in the service statement comprising Section 2 of the Agreement.

Other services

If there are other services in which the LIS is involved, such as partnerships with other organizations, then these need to be included, perhaps as a separate part of the SLA. Draw attention to any electronic services; we expand on dealing with these in Chapter 10.

Value-added tax

Regardless of the absence (in the UK) of VAT on publications, a number of the services that the LIS purchases will have VAT levied on part or all of the sums paid. Some obvious examples are CDs, whether CD-ROMs or sound recordings; online databases; photocopies; and subscriptions (which – like books with CDs enclosed – may be complicated by having VAT on only a part of the invoice).

The SLA therefore needs to have some terms in it relating to the way in which VAT is handled. In addition to the terms set out here, you may wish to include something to indicate the way in which accounting is to be handled, specifying whether the VAT amount is to be deducted from other monies handed over, or whether any sums passed between the customer and the supplier will have VAT included in full.

> **The budget shall not be debited with any VAT chargeable on the supply of services provided in accordance with the Agreement and recoverable by the organization under its agreements with HM Customs and Excise, and HM Treasury.**

> **Where consent has been given under Section 4 of this Annexe, the subcontract will include provision for VAT to be paid to the subcontractor in addition to the budget, which will include the subcontract price, and a sum equal to the VAT chargeable on the value of supply of goods and services provided in accordance with the subcontract.**

Resolution of disputes

We pointed out in the previous chapter that it is unwise to have a single point of resolution for disputes at too high a level within the company or organization, in order to avoid the possibility of a senior manager making an isolated decision in dispute with him or herself as the head of two or more management chains. It is sensible to include the final phrase of the next contract statement, in order to close off an endless series of potential appeals.

This is also a good place to include details of escalation procedures. These are laid down in the agreement, setting out the route that is to be pursued by a customer with a dispute, before the final authority of the head of office services (or someone of similar standing) is invoked. Having these named contacts available is reassuring to the customer. It shows not only that the service is being taken seriously by the supplier, but it also makes it clear to the LIS managers away from the workface that they have a responsibility for customer satisfaction.

It is not a good idea to identify by name the people in the escalation chain. Agreements that follow this path lapse on a technicality each time a named person changes post within the organization (and is thus no longer within the relevant management path) or leaves the organization. The post, but not the postholder, should be identified. You can always provide details of the names in an annexe or separate update; by doing this you avoid having to ask for change control or asking the customer's approval every time LIS staff moves take place.

In the first instance all disputes, differences or questions between the parties to the Agreement shall be referred to the XYZ LIS initial contact point(s) shown in Table 1 of Annexe W. For the customer, these contact points shall be as set out in Table 2. If the problem is not resolved, an escalation procedure shall be started and the problem resolved to the next level or levels as shown in the Table.

Any disputes, differences or questions between the parties to the Agreement with respect to any matter arising out of or relating to the

29

> Agreement (other than where the decision of the customer or a named
> individual is, under the Agreement, to be final, and except to the extent
> where special provision for resolution is made elsewhere in the Agree-
> ment) and remaining unresolved by the escalation procedure set out in
> the section above shall be referred to the director of office services [or
> someone fulfilling a similar function] whose decision shall be final.

Default

The agreement needs to spell out what is to happen if the LIS defaults on
its service to the extent that the customer cancels all or part of the service.
The client side may make assumptions about its powers to close the service
(with consequent inconvenience to the users), based on factors such as the
severity of the breakdown, the speed with which it can be closed, and the re-
tendering of the service. There may also be assumptions about the funding
available during a period of notice, just as there may be librarians who maintain lists of expensive titles to be purchased by an LIS team who are removed
midway through a financial year! The best plan is to spell everything out in
detail.

You may be able to include a clause about the continuing employment of
LIS staff in this situation if they are members of the client company staff. For
example, you will probably want to preserve their employment rights under
a new contractor, or ensure that they will be reabsorbed into the main organization if new contractors bring their own staff into the LIS.

> If the services or any portion thereof are not carried out in accordance
> with the specification, the customer may cancel the Agreement [by giv-
> ing 00 days' notice of cancellation, which may be withdrawn during the
> period of notice]. In this case, the in-house team will continue to provide
> a service (but no longer under the terms of this Agreement) until the end
> of the notice period or until such time as a starting date has been agreed
> for alternative arrangements.

> The LIS budget will continue to be available as agreed during the period of notice and there will be no change to the conditions and terms of service of the staff of XYZ LIS during any such period of notice.

Duty of care

The client side can reasonably expect a statement on the duty of care, addressing the skills required to carry out the terms of the agreement. For the LIS contract, it would be appropriate to make reference to The Library Association's *Code of professional conduct*[1] or a similar document. Here or elsewhere in the agreement it would be useful to include commitments to training and continuing professional development. Where these are bound into a corporate agreement it is considerably easier to give the funds to provide them a high priority in the budget. At the same time, care needs to be exercised to avoid committing to a level of quality in an area that is outside the LIS's control, for example the accuracy of databases.

> The LIS shall be responsible for ensuring that reasonable skill, care and diligence are exercised in carrying out the services properly and efficiently in accordance with the Agreement.
>
> All tasks shall be carried out in the most efficient and workmanlike manner to the entire satisfaction of the customer.
>
> Professional staff will comply with the requirements of The Library Association's *Code of professional conduct* to be 'competent in professional activities [and keep abreast of developments in librarianship]'.
>
> Despite the provisions laid out above, the LIS gives no guarantee of the accuracy of information supplied by third parties (e.g. in publications, databases, etc.), unless the customer specifically requests at the time of ordering that information should be verified against further sources before supply, or a measure of reliability supplied.

Hours of work

You will probably want to make a number of statements about the hours of service, hours of work, and what happens in an emergency, or about other requirements for extended working. It is worthwhile thinking through what major events could happen that would need an LIS presence. In a number of cases in the public sector, the unthinkable has happened and LIS staff have been to the fore. For example, LIS staff are more accustomed than many people to dealing continuously with the public, and in handling people who are trying urgently to find information. Reference interview techniques could be invaluable here. Offer the LIS's services if appropriate, after finding out, of course, if your staff are willing to work the necessary hours to cope with such a crisis. (Also think of how they are going to reach the office in an emergency, if that is a likely problem.)

We deal with the definition of service hours, and exceptions to those hours, in Chapter 4, but it is in this quasicontractual part of the agreement that you should insert any general statements or terms and conditions, allowing you to put detailed information in an annexe to the SLA, where it can be adjusted more easily than in the main document. The wording of the first suggested contract statement below allows for this adjustment at short notice (e.g. to cover unexpected staff absences), and could be expressed in hours rather than days if this is appropriate. The same wording will also allow for extra working in an emergency, and does not tie either side down to a definition of an emergency. In Chapter 4 we have given some conditions, which, in practice, may prevent or have prevented LIS from giving a full service. The definition of conditions needing extra service are likely to be individual to each organization.

> LIS services will be available at the times and on the conditions listed in Annexe U, which may be amended by the parties to this agreement by mutual consent at 00 days' [or hours'] notice.

> If the LIS staff members wish to work outside normal working hours for their own benefit, any additional costs for this will be debited to the Agreed Budget.

> **Any additional costs for hours worked at the sole instigation of the customer (including expenses incurred by LIS staff in providing a remote service outside normal working hours in support of the customer) shall be debited to a budget or budgets controlled by the customer.**

Occupation of premises

As has been mentioned earlier, the agreement with the LIS may well state that accommodation is provided free of charge, and that heating, lighting, telephones, data points, Integrated Services Digital Network (ISDN) and other services are included. If payment is required, real or notional, here is the place to state what is included, so that the end of year party is not disrupted by the arrival of a large bill for telephones or for the ISDN link, which the organization had assumed was an LIS responsibility because nobody else in the building had one.

> **The costs of using land or premises (including temporary buildings) made available to the LIS shall be charged to the Agreed Budget or to a sub-budget. Any utilities required by the LIS shall be included in such charges to the Agreed Budget.**

LIS organization

These clauses feature in a number of agreements. In the case of the points below you should consider whether this wording is acceptable, or whether a period of notice should be required. Some customer organizations assume that they have the right to cut the budget of an SLA-managed unit in-year, just as they would any directly managed unit in the event of budget reductions. If the company is on the verge of bankruptcy, the argument is probably academic, but, in a large organization, it may be worth insisting that changes cannot be made except on agreed review dates.

The final point is a useful one when the tender documentation has relied heavily on the experience of one or more members of staff, or where their skills are seen as crucial to the operation of the LIS. Quite apart from staff moving to other jobs, they do fall ill or decide to retire to the tranquillity of the countryside. For the remaining staff to find themselves in breach of their SLA as a result is unacceptable.

> **The LIS shall provide and maintain an organization having the necessary facilities to undertake the tasks specified in the schedules and specifications.**
>
> **If as a result of changes to the budget or other funding, alterations are necessary to the level of service available, the LIS will consult with the customer to agree a mutually acceptable revised service level.**
>
> **This Agreement does not identify any key personnel.**

Facilities provided

In addition to the paragraphs suggested here, there should be a statement about the provision of services such as electricity and water supplies. In an office environment, which is likely to rely heavily on information technology (IT), it would be as well to point firmly at the legislation on working conditions because of the heat generated by computers and peripherals. You may consider it excessive to state a maximum temperature for the workspace but issues as apparently trivial as this have the capability to bring an LIS to a halt and tempers to unsuspected heights.

> **Common areas of the organization's buildings will not be charged against the Agreed Budget; only those facilities identified in standard costings will be charged.**
>
> **Common services will be provided to the LIS and these will normally be used, for example, for delivery of information to customers. Any additional costs (e.g. for courier services) will be met by the customer.**

Continuity of electricity and water supplies is not guaranteed by the client, but, where this affects the ability of the LIS to provide services the provisions of Annexe T shall apply. [See Chapter 4 for further details.]

Duration of agreement

A statement about the duration of the agreement is highly recommended. This works in two ways. Certainly, it gives the client the right to terminate the agreement early, but its main purpose is to set out its expected length, which should probably be three or five years. The second clause gives the option to extend a successful agreement without the need to go to the expense and inconvenience of a new tender operation. The option date should give at least six months' notice.

This Agreement shall commence on [date] and shall remain in force until [date], subject to the customer's right of earlier termination under the sections of the Agreement.

The customer also reserves the right to extend the Agreement beyond the period stated in the specification. Adjustments to the Agreed Budget will be agreed between the customer and the LIS. The extension will be for a minimum of 12 months and such options will be exercised by the customer on or before [date].

Transfer of responsibility

These clauses are likely to appear in some form or other in an agreement. While the first one clearly protects the organization's interests, the second is a reasonable trade-off.

If a different organization is required to take on the service at the expiry or termination of the Agreement, the LIS shall co-operate in the transfer.

The transfer shall be arranged to reduce to a minimum any interruption in the services.

If the responsibilities of the LIS are transferred to another organization during the lifetime of this agreement, these terms and conditions shall be considered as a specification.

Variations of requirement

There has to be some condition in the agreement allowing the parties to vary the terms. The wording here allows the customer to vary the requirement, which is the most likely event, but the LIS may wish to add a further clause allowing it to propose changes to the requirement in the light of emerging patterns of use, or new services. (Remember that an LIS signing an unalterable five-year agreement in 1992 would have had no way of introducing the internet, which, by 1997, would have been a considerable handicap.)

Building review meetings into the agreement ensures that there is a means of communication, allowing not only for the customer to raise service issues with the LIS but also for the LIS staff to bring new and potentially useful services to the client's attention.

The customer reserves the right to vary the requirements of the Agreement as detailed in the specification should this at any time become necessary. In the event of any variation in the Agreement requirement, adjustments to the Agreed Budget will be agreed between the customer and the LIS.

Nominated representatives of the customer and the LIS will meet at least every six months to consider new service possibilities and costings, and to agree any variations under paragraph 0.0 above that may be required as a result.

Meetings to vary the requirements of the Agreement above may be called by either party at seven days' notice.

Technical clauses

We now come to a number of technical clauses, which you would be well advised to include.

Agreement documents

> In case of any discrepancy between these sections and other documents forming part of the Agreement, these sections prevail.

Amendments to agreement

> In case of any discrepancy between these sections and other documents forming part of the Agreement, these sections prevail.

Monitoring and liaison meetings

Apart from meetings to deal with contractual issues and potential new services, liaison is needed to ensure that the current requirements are being met. These sections provide for such meetings, which as the text says, do not have to be separate. Since most of the players will be the same, these could be further agenda items at the same gathering as the service reviews.

> The LIS shall be responsible for monitoring its performance of the Agreement and shall provide the customer with full particulars of any aspects of its performance that fail to meet the requirements of the Agreement.
>
> Liaison meetings between the LIS and the customer shall be held as required by either party, in addition to the meetings described above to consider new services (although these meetings need not be separate).

> A record of all meetings shall be made by the LIS and copies provided to the customer.

Price

Price is clearly an important element, especially as many SLAs arise out of a desire by the corporate body to control the costs of its LIS. We shall discuss charging in more detail later, but here are some suggested clauses for this part of the agreement.

> Unless otherwise stated in the Schedules, the Agreed Budget shall not be exceeded by the LIS and shall be considered to be the total budget out of which the services are to be provided.

> Before supplies of publications purchased on subscription are renewed, or other committed expenditure is made, the LIS shall consult the customer and indicate whether the Agreed Budget is likely to be sufficient.

> If it is decided to extend the term of the Agreement or to change the scope of the Agreement, the Agreed Budget will be amended, the amount of such amendment to be agreed between the customer and the LIS.

Allocation of costs

This is a simple but necessary statement. You may wish to include a statement about the procedure to be followed at the end of the financial year, or state the day of each month on which the debit will take place. Depending on the arrangements for repaying credits, you may also need a statement to the effect that credits are returned to the LIS budget and not to be applied to any central account for incoming payments.

> The costs of providing the services will be debited against the Allocated Budget monthly. Credits from suppliers will be applied to the Allocated

> Budget from which they were originally debited, and will increase the
> funds then available.

Billing arrangements

As we discuss in the section on charging, invoices may be either notional or intended for payment. In the case of notional invoices, use the wording in paragraph 1. If the invoices are intended for payment, the words 'notional' and 'for information' should be removed, and wording added such as that in the second paragraph.

> The LIS will prepare notional invoices and present these to the customer
> at two-monthly intervals for information, no more than one month in
> arrears at the end of the accounting period.
>
> All invoices shall be paid in full by the customer within 30 days, unless
> agreement has been reached with the LIS in case of a dispute or query.

Service First

The original Citizen's Charter concept in the UK has been gradually modified, so that although many, including a number of the early recipients, continue to view the Charter Mark as a reward for excellence, the scheme has gradually become focused on encouraging improvement in public service delivery.[2] The scheme extends to charities, contractors and companies as well as the more obvious areas of the public sector such as central and local government, and the health and emergency services.

This means that the processes for achieving the Charter Mark are becoming more closely aligned with the methods of service level agreement management. If your organization intends to achieve a Charter Mark, or indeed aspires to other schemes that are intended to mark the quality of or improvements to service delivery, then a section such as this should appear in your SLA:

This Agreement is fully consistent with the aim of the Service First Charter Mark to encourage improvement in public service delivery. To achieve this end a number of objectives will be met that reflect Charter Mark principles, in particular publishing performance standards, consultation with users and suppliers, achieving best value, consumer empowerment and improving the quality of services provided. These specific objectives are as follows:

- A user committee will meet at quarterly intervals chaired by the Head of Corporate Services and with members from the Research Department, Production Management and Customer Services.
- A summary of service standards will be posted in all library and information service points.
- Information on XXX [insert your subject area] will be provided to the levels stated in Appendix D.
- The LIS will maintain and deliver a comprehensive records management service meeting [standard] by 2004.

Third-party partnership

Your LIS's success in achieving some of its aims is dependent on obtaining commitment from its third-party partners and related services (e.g. information systems department, photocopying, transport and postal services, and other information services on whom you call). All of the standards set out in your agreement will therefore be met only if a successful partnership is achieved. You should consider the following paragraph.

XYZ LIS and its customers and related services operate a successful partnership. Where the provision of the services is dependent on the actions of a third party or parties outwith the direct control of the supplier, then the supplier shall not be held accountable for service failures resulting from such actions, or failure to take action, of these third parties. Nevertheless, the supplier is required, wherever possible, to take appropriate

action to mitigate any service failures that do occur and, as far as is practicable, to reduce the likelihood of their re-occurrence.

Summary

You will probably consider that the above is a somewhat daunting list, but, once you have these items sorted out and agreed, then your SLA should work to all the parties' satisfaction. Chapter 4 will take you into the further details that are needed in your SLA. You should not worry too much at this stage of SLA development; it does take time to draw the document together, but this guidance should make life a little easier! Remember, you are in control, and getting it right will be worth the pain now, rather than having problems later.

Points on which to reflect

- Make sure your definitions are understood by your customer.
- Ensure that you check out all the items listed above for possible inclusion in your own SLA.
- Add to and develop the sections above depending on your LIS's circumstances.

4

What the SLA document should look like and descriptions of services

---

In this chapter you will find:

- a format outline of an SLA document
- sample descriptions of services
- sample statements of service availability
- sample statements of delivery of LIS materials and services.

Format of the SLA document

In the previous chapter we looked at the general conditions of contract and other prefatory material that you might wish or need to include in your SLA. In this chapter we look at questions more closely related to the LIS, and suggest a model format for the SLA, with a commentary on each section. As for the previous chapter, your local circumstances will affect the elements you include and the exact wording you choose.

The SLA document should contain in the introduction a statement of the format of the document. In this way, your customer, the receiver of the service, knows exactly what to find. In this chapter we suggest and explore the following format:

- conditions and definitions for the agreement (see Chapter 3)
- general description of the services available from the LIS
- schedule of the services from within that general description that the

agreement provides to the customer group or division in an organization
- definitions or glossary of terms used in the document
- annexes giving details of, for example
  — general conditions of the contract
  — help desks or contact name, telephone numbers, etc.
  — schedules of additional sources agreed with the customer
  — services to the public
  — change control procedure, etc., giving the date of the document.

General description of available services

In this section we suggest the elements that should be included in a statement of the range of services available from the LIS. Customers will select from the range, so this list should be comprehensive. The following general information and basic details might be used for a special LIS. They could be adapted for academic or public use, and public librarians (and others) can also draw usefully upon The Library Association's model standards document.[1]

Delivery points

Location details of the information centre or LIS should be stated, so that it is clear which operations are covered by the SLA. When these locations are listed and identified in the organization's internal directory, it is simple enough to refer to this; otherwise they will need to be set out in the document. Listing these in an annexe reduces change control problems, and allows any alterations to locations to be published as an office notice.

If there are any restrictions on the use of particular libraries (e.g. a legal collection, which may be reserved for, or for which first call is given to lawyers), this is the place to include that information.

Now that there is an increase in homeworking, consideration needs to be given to what exactly constitutes a 'delivery point'. It may be that, because of the type of work carried out by the end-user, research, access to databases and SDI services will be needed more by the individual user than by a section within the organization. So this must be included in the description of the SLA.

Standard LIS services

Here you will need to state quite firmly what are considered to be the basic, or standard, services. A typical statement would run along the lines of the following:

> **Answering enquiries on all subjects of interest to organization XYZ based on collections of publications held as reference material and/or for lending at the main LIS and branch libraries, and using external sources to support these collections.**

Here you could state what the LIS aims to provide, for example:

> **The XYZ LIS aims to provide and promote an information and loans service for organization XYZ.**
>
> **It also provides an enquiry service on XYZ organizational matters for members of the public, as described in paragraph 0.0 and subsequent references from that paragraph.**

Also state here if the LIS provides professional support and some facilities to other linked organizations, for example, to other companies within the group or to associated charities, or in support of other local authority services.

Current awareness service

When a current awareness service is provided, based on the regular production and circulation of a list of recently acquired LIS materials likely to be of interest to customers (e.g. based on the organization's interests or reflecting the interests of divisions in a given building), a description should be inserted. Include statements of:

- *Availability*: is this available organization-wide, or to particular divisions or departments?
- *Format*: is a paper copy available to certain groups of users only, the remainder perhaps having to use a bulletin board or receive e-mail copies?
- *Frequency*: state the frequency and time of publication and note any exceptions (e.g. at public holiday times).

A statement can be also be made about available related and complementary internal or external services.

Loan of LIS material

Describe the service of lending documents from the LIS stock to customers in the organization for pre-set and notified durations of time.

If different time periods apply to different groups (e.g. faculty, senior management), these should be set out here. Put the details in an annexe to avoid the need for change control.

> **The loan periods are set out in Annexe Z and may be varied by three months' notice to the LIS committee. LIS materials not required by another reader may be renewed but must be produced for checking at every fourth renewal.**

Document supply

The terminology used by LIS varies considerably and the definition of a 'document' used by your LIS may be wider than that used here. There needs to be included some statement that makes clear the terms on which documents are supplied. It should be made particularly obvious that the LIS operates only on these terms, so that accepting a document supplied by the LIS binds the user to respect the intellectual property rights in it: copyright for printed materials, and performing and other rights in videos, software and multimedia items.

The supply of photocopies of extracts from documents in the LIS's stock, regulated by the provisions of the law of copyright, and the additional provisions of the licence from the Copyright Licensing Agency held by the LIS.

The supply of extracts from documents held in remote databases by commercial and other suppliers, and regulated by agreements in force concerning the copyright in those documents.

Consider the implications of more full text being available directly to the end user. The LIS will need to ensure that the data is copyright cleared before offering such services. In Chapter 10 we suggest that this work should be carried out by the e-suppliers.

Information retrieval

Many users are probably unaware that you obtain material from other databases, despite your best efforts to promote the service! Give yourself the right to do so. If the organization has a policy about connection to external services, this is where it should be picked up; for example, there might be concerns about intelligence being gleaned from the search terms you are using, or you might need improved and more secure lines.

The retrieval and presentation of selected records taken from remote computer-held databases of information, or from databases on CD-ROM held in the LIS. Unless otherwise specified in Annexe Y, searches are carried out in the LIS by information staff using details provided by the customer.

Selective dissemination of information

Many LIS offer SDI services of one form or another; these may vary from one customer group to another. The service should be defined, together with any riders identifying any services restricted to certain groups of users. If these restrictions are for the duration of the agreement, they are inserted here; if they are going to change, or are likely to change, they should be detailed in an annexe.

> A service providing current information from the LIS's database(s), or from external databases, to selected customers or groups of customers in the departments, by matching the indexing terms of newly published materials with the search profiles of customers.

Interlibrary loans

> Loans of material borrowed from elsewhere, arranged through the XYZ LIS for its customers.

You may wish to add a note about any limits on the number of loans per section or per person at any one time. This is a section of definitions rather than conditions of use, but note our remarks in Chapter 7 on managing the customer. You should ensure that your users are aware of the restrictions that apply to you, and insist that they bring back your loans on time.

Purchase of publications

Many LIS act as the intelligent purchasers of publications across their organizations, not just for their own stock. This wording defines this service, and adds some restrictions to make it clear that the LIS retains control of the budget. You may wish to consider some extra details if your budget is limited from the outset, or if you have a budget to spend on behalf of other divisions in an organization.

> The purchase and provision for use within organization XYZ of documents specified by customers for purposes that make the provision of a loan copy or copies inappropriate, but subject to any restrictions on supply brought about by the LIS budgetary management, and otherwise at the LIS's discretion.

Abstracting

In organizations such as research bodies, the LIS may write abstracts of the literature entering the organization and add this to an LIS or organization-wide database. This definition may also be useful if the research teams compile abstracts as part of their work and expect income from the abstracts when used by the rest of the organization.

> Making and recording on the LIS database a summary of the information in a document that has been catalogued and/or indexed in the LIS.

Cataloguing

A definition of cataloguing is useful not only for the work done by the LIS, but also when a separate section creates records relating to a special collection. The standards should preferably be universally recognized. Typically, the Anglo-American Cataloguing Rules (AACR2) should be used, and the level of detail within the Rules stated, but otherwise there should be a defined and measurable standard against which compliance can be examined.

> The creation of bibliographic records according to stated and agreed standards and their incorporation into the LIS database.

Indexing

Similarly, indexing standards need to be established within the SLA. It may be necessary in the schedule or in an annexe to state whose responsibility it is to provide the thesaurus used. Clearly, there is a wide difference in start-up costs between running off a further copy of an in-house thesaurus, or providing access to its database, and that of purchasing a set of Library of Congress subject headings.

> **The creation or enhancement of bibliographic records with terms from the indexing language listed in the LIS thesaurus (or other agreed sources) in order to allow their later retrieval for current awareness or in response to enquiries.**

Circulation of periodicals (circulation management)

Many LIS will circulate periodicals within the organization. The restrictions or conditions on this service can be set out in detail in a later section, and any lists of titles should go in another annexe.

> **The distribution through [internal] mail services of consecutive issues of periodicals to users named in sequence on a list compiled from requests to view copies on circulation that have been agreed by the XYZ LIS.**

With the availability of the electronic journal the LIS will need to ensure that only those with agreed access should be allowed the password to e-journals. It maybe that the agreement is for all the organization to have access to a set of e-journals. The LIS will need to ensure that the agreement with the e-journal agent reflects this. See Chapter 10 for further details. Bear in mind the variations in costs.

> **The access to agreed e-journals including the table of contents, full text, archive files to named users will be arranged through the LIS.**

The LIS will need to ascertain from the user group if they will need access to electronically held archives of journals. The LIS may have decided that the print holdings within the LIS should satisfy the users, but if arrangements are to be made with the e-suppliers for electronic access to archive files then this should be part of the agreement with them.

> **The access to agreed e-journals archives to named users will be arranged through the LIS.**

Binding

A binding service may be provided by some LIS. The exact wording will of course reflect the work done (e.g. collation, minor repair work, etc.).

> **Preparation of the organizational material for binding or rebinding by a chosen external contractor.**

Disposal of publications

You should have the right to dispose of documents no longer required by the LIS, which may otherwise involve the LIS in wastage in terms of storage costs and staff time involved in keeping the stock. It may be necessary to include further defining text, for example if the LIS holds material as part of a co-operative, particularly where this entails holding items that would otherwise be judged fit for disposal.

Advisory services

A statement defining professional advisory services can be useful, not least as a means of advertising the skills of the LIS staff beyond the purely custodial role that many observers believe to be the limit of their value.

> **Advice to the organization's departments on the indexing of publications, and the organization and classification of collections of publications or of other information resources held within departments.**

Copyright advice

Here, you need to be trained and constantly updated to be able to answer or obtain answers to copyright queries from both within the organization and from the public. A reference to the copyright acts and related secondary legislation may be required here. The reference to LIS privileges establishes further reason for the LIS to lay claim to this area of work.

> **Advice to the organization's departments on aspects of copying from published sources and on LIS privileges. Administration of the photocopying licences to the organization from the Copyright Licensing Agency, the Newspaper Licensing Agency and the Ordnance Survey, and advice to departments on licensed copying. Administration of the system for multiple copying from copyright materials.**
>
> **Taking further legal or other advice as required, advice on Crown copyright [i.e. an acknowledgement that Crown and Parliamentary copyrights are difficult areas where the LIS may need standing agreements to incur expenses by seeking professional legal advice, consulting government departments or contacting the residual HMSO in order to give proper advice].**

In the section concerned with customer responsibilities you will need to make reference to your users' responsibility to observe copyright in materials provided from your LIS. This section is solely concerned with defining your services.

Sales of the organization's publications

If you are the sales point for the organization, wording such as this will define the role. If the LIS does not fulfil this role and does not wish to take it on, it may still be appropriate to make the reference to knowledge of the publishing output of the organization.

> Where specified in Annexe ZZ to this Agreement, the sales of and accounting for publications by the organization.
>
> To maintain a database of publications by organization XYZ and to provide details of these publications to callers/members of the public.

Additional information and LIS services

If you provide additional services, these need to be specified here with the appropriate level of detail. Services may include database management, records and archive services, technical and computer management, or directory compilation.

In a public or academic LIS, other services will be offered, and the performance indicators proposed in the Department of National Heritage's consultation paper *Reading the future*[2] include accounting for issues of audio-cassettes (music and spoken word), CD-ROMs and computer software, so definitions of these services may well be required, with supporting statements of availability and service standards placed later in the document. Online and electronic media are also proposed as access and usage categories, so the detail suggested here may need to be further developed.

Service availability

In this section we suggest some clauses that will set the description of services into some local context. The next essential step following these descriptions is to state when and where the service will be available, the activities at each of the locations used by the LIS, and some statements of times at which the service will be unavailable, whether by design or because of some other conditions that make the LIS unavailable or unusable for some reason. A priority must be to ensure that, if the LIS is out of action through a situation beyond its control, it cannot be held to be in breach of its agreements.

LIS services will normally be available Monday to Friday from 09.15 to 17.30 [or whatever days of the week and times are agreed], or, in branch LIS, at such other times as displayed or agreed with customers and recorded in Annexe XY to this Agreement. The service point may, at the discretion of the head of the LIS or other officer in charge, pass the enquiry (request, etc.) to another service point for completion.

Services may be available outside these hours either by telephone or personal call to other LIS service points. Telephone numbers are listed in Annexe YY to this Agreement and are shown on the LIS's publicity materials.

Services may be curtailed or suspended on the occurrence of one or more of the following events:

(a) any breakdown in building facilities and utilities (including computer systems, whether or not maintained by LIS) making it impossible to access information services;

(b) suspension or curtailment of public transport services affecting the area;

(c) any trades dispute affecting LIS staff or service provided to the LIS, including those affecting originators, providers, carriers or deliverers of information and documents;

(d) any breakdown in building facilities and utilities making it impossible to maintain safe, hygienic or tolerable working conditions within the terms of the Offices Shops and Railway Premises Act 1963, the Health and Safety at Work etc. Act 1974, or any other relevant legislation from time to time in force;

(e) public holidays, privilege holidays or other days on which the organization is otherwise closed for business;

(f) closure or evacuation of the building, or part of the building occupied by the LIS or its stock.

In these cases, apart from (e), best endeavours will be made to provide a service or to produce copies of documents from other sources, but no guarantee can be given. In cases of national or regional crisis or emergency, a weekend service may be provided by arrangement, but this agreement will be suspended for the duration of the supply of any such services.

A report in the form shown below will be supplied at monthly intervals detailing any interruptions to the service lasting for more than two working hours as a result of any of the events listed in sections (a), (b), (c), (d) or (f) above.

You will need to ensure that this part of the SLA is constantly revisited and amended. Any new legislation affecting conditions in offices or other premises used by the LIS will have to be included. (We look at other relevant legislation later in this book; here we are concerned solely with legislation relating to the use of buildings.)

You will already be supplying a considerable amount of information to your customer and this can quite easily be included on the form. With luck the report will be routine, apart from the odd bank holiday and fire drill. However, this can be quite a serious point. When organizations that observe different public holidays supply services to one another some bizarre situations can arise. Organizations with offices in Scotland will find this a strong likelihood, as there are not only different bank holidays from England, Wales and Northern Ireland but also some local holidays observed in particular cities.

Case study

In one instance, the only workers in a building owned by organization C were the telephone operators supplied by organization K, which observed a different additional day's holiday at Christmas. When organization C's employees returned to work, they found that the switchboard was unmanned, as organization K had added an extra day's holiday at New Year.

Some wording is needed, finally, to allow for the locking or otherwise of the LIS at night, and for allowing your trusted customers the occasional use of reference books overnight.

Access to the LIS room(s) will normally be available outside the hours stated, but this is not guaranteed. LIS materials normally restricted to the LIS room(s) may exceptionally be provided on short-term loan in order to make them available outside the hours stated at the discretion of the head of the LIS or the officer in charge.

---

e-enquiry service

The '24 x 7 society' makes increasing demands that the LIS must consider, and decide whether and how it will meet them. There are a number of good examples showing how enquiry services can be delivered round the clock.

- A United Kingdom university information service links with a partner service in a New Zealand university to provide an e-reference enquiry service. Each provides enquirers with an e-mail address that can be used outside their own service hours, and the reply will come from either New Zealand or the UK directly to the enquirer, depending on the time that the enquiry is finally resolved. A 24-hour service is thus made available without the need to pay for 24-hour staffing.
- A number of multinational companies build on the fact that one of their major offices with professional library and information services is open somewhere around the world at any given time. For example, a European, North American and Asian office can each progress enquiries during their own opening hours, and pass the research to the next office at the end of the local working day. The enquirer will receive a response, signed off by the office that completed the research, but representing the corporate library and information service worldwide.

This is all good sense and an innovative use of technology, but it requires your SLA to cover any such services, stating:

- the ways in which these e-enquiry services operate
- who can use the service (for example defining the limits of the organization and whether local customers enjoy any priority over those on other campuses or even in other countries)
- when it is available (which may be a statement of continuous service where service in person is not required or where it is provided by e-mail out of local working hours)
- who assumes responsibility for the quality and progress of enquiries
- how service will be monitored, including the person or persons to whom the reports will be delivered.

Delivery of LIS materials and services

We now move to a number of general statements regarding the delivery of services and documents to the customer. After a preamble signalling that these conditions apply to the internal service, a number of statements are suggested that express the LIS's goodwill and its general approach to its service. The following statements relate to services provided to members of the organization. Services to the general public are as stated later in this document.

At least one professional librarian information specialist is normally available at each service point during the hours listed in Annexe B. At other times professional staff may be available at one or other LIS site.

The LIS will use all its resources, both internal and external, to meet customers' requirements within the constraints of time, economy and staffing.

Requests for access to published books, periodicals, reports, official publications, audiovisual materials, maps, standards, etc. ('publications')

> will be assessed by the LIS staff and copies provided for loan or reten-
> tion, from stock, by purchase order, or by borrowing from other
> collections as appropriate. Requests may be made by telephone, in per-
> son, in writing, or by electronic mail. Customers will provide such
> information as is available to assist the LIS staff or their suppliers in trac-
> ing correctly the bibliographic description and location of publications.

The next paragraph regulates the re-use of copyright material and could demonstrate the LIS's determination to observe the law in the case of a discovered breach. It may need to be reinforced by a statement regarding fair dealing and any other areas of company or LIS policy on copying. Obviously, it will need to be amended in the light of the licences held.

> All LIS material supplied for use by customers is provided subject to the
> law of copyright and the terms of the licences to the XYZ organization
> from the Copyright Licensing Agency, the Newspaper Licensing Agency
> and the Ordnance Survey, of Crown or Parliamentary copyright, or of any
> more specific restrictions applying to other materials such as unpublished
> theses. Materials supplied to LIS customers may not be further copied or
> otherwise used outside the provisions of copyright law as extended by
> the licences held for the XYZ organization.

You may wish to give your LIS a stated right to use electronic services in the first instance; indeed, some organizations will look quite favourably on this approach. This paragraph also provides some kind of indication to the organization of the level of technical support and the systems capacity required (bandwidth and the maximum size of file that can be sent safely across the office network). We have also used the opportunity again to make a statement about copyright, this time to insist that copyright notices and provenance tags in electronic records should not be removed.

> The LIS will use electronic information retrieval systems wherever appro-
> priate or when significant savings in cost or effort appear possible. The

> results of such searches will be delivered by electronic mail wherever they are available in a form suitable for transmission by this means to a mailbox currently available to the customer. Files delivered in this way may not be further used other than for printing out. In particular, they may not be stored in electronic form for further use with retrieval software unless a specific request for the required clearance has been made at the time of ordering and the head of the LIS has indicated that the appropriate fee has been paid. All copyright notices and other provenance markings attached to electronic files must be retained unaltered with the data to which they refer.

The following statement may need to be reinforced for senior management customers!

> When there is a deadline, every effort will be made to meet it.

You will, however, still need to give yourself some leeway:

> LIS staff will endeavour to provide services as quickly as possible. Answering machines may be used to provide a telephone service at busy times and recorded requests will be answered or acknowledged within four working hours or any shorter deadline agreed with the customer.

The next conditions are both of great importance. The first relates to the accuracy of information retrieved, whether online or in print. Exhaustive searching and double-checking, which is not necessarily the norm in many LIS, may represent an additional service, and a higher charge may be made as a result.

> Information provided will be accurate and material held will be as up to date as is available. Where it is essential that an exhaustive search for information takes place, the customer should inform the librarian when the request is placed. However, the LIS does not warrant that the material is fully accurate unless a specific request has been made to that

> effect and a warranty given to XYZ organization. It follows that neither the LIS nor its suppliers will be liable for the accuracy of information unless such a warranty has been specifically given to the user.

The next condition is to safeguard both the LIS and the customer against computer viruses. There is more on this in the section regarding customer responsibilities.

> The customer must be personally satisfied that any electronic media supplied are free from virus infection. While the LIS will check all media before use, no guarantee is given, especially not in respect of any media supplied by a third party (e.g. with a book or periodical subscription).

Now, we suggest some statements that are more specifically connected with the handling of enquiries and the provision of an LIS collection.

> A comprehensive collection of material relevant to customers' information needs will be maintained. Customer needs will be systematically surveyed at intervals of 00 months.

> Copies of the LIS Collection Development Policy will be provided on request in connection with this initiative.

You will need to ensure that appropriate mechanisms, including the allocation of staff time, are in place to be able to carry out this function.

The next statement relates to the competence of both professional and paraprofessional LIS staff, and represents a commitment to training. It may be appropriate, depending on the organization's policy, to include reference to S/NVQs or *The investors in people standard* [3] (widely adopted in business, government and other organizations which place emphasis on the value of training), or to the use of a professional scheme such as The Library Association's professional development profile [4] or the profiles contained in the British Computer Society's *Industry structure model*. [5]

LIS staff will be trained appropriately to use LIS resources. The customer's staff will be guided in the use of LIS resources (tours, demonstrations) at the beginning of this agreement and thereafter on request.

Turnaround times

Now we will set out some suggested turnaround times. The service specification contained in tender documents may impose a more complicated structure than this, involving different standards for different customers (e.g. a one-hour response for senior management). If the time to respond is set out in an invitation-to-tender document, it may be possible to refer to this, but it may be most satisfactory to repeat the service levels within the SLA document. Unless the times are varied at each review, it is reasonable to place this information in the body of the agreement rather than in an annexe.

Enquiries from the organization's staff will be responded to within one working day. Enquiries expected to take longer than this will be carried out within an agreed timetable. Enquirers will be kept informed of progress.

A final paragraph in this section should deal with services to the public. It may be appropriate to include copies of the form letters used to handle public enquiries in an annexe.

Enquiries from members of the public that fall within the agreed parameters for LIS services (stated in Annexe D to this agreement, as and if amended by Annexe C) will be answered as quickly as possible. A response will be given to all telephone enquiries within one working day. The LIS will try to answer these enquiries from its own resources and, if it cannot help, try to suggest an alternative source of information. Ninety per cent of written enquiries will be answered within ten working days. Letters that cannot be answered within these limits will be acknowl-

edged. Enquiries falling outside the current parameters for service will receive a courteous note within five working days referring them to public libraries or other appropriate sources.

Loans

The next function to be included is loans. We suggest a possible approach, although again there may be more complex standards than this where particular user groups are entitled to a higher (or lower) level of service.

All requests will be responded to either by: (a) the despatch of the available publication within two working days; or (b) an acknowledgement of the request, together with a statement of the action taken and an estimate of the expected delivery date.

When delivery is not possible within six months (e.g. because of the delayed publication of a new title, or heavy demand for a scarce publication), the LIS will consult the issuer of the request to determine what further action should be taken.

Clearly, some kind of monitoring process will be required to ensure that the deadlines are met. It is also wise to indicate to the customer those areas over which the LIS has control and those that are in the hands of the book trade or publishers. However, a commitment such as the following will make the LIS's role clearer.

Publications that have waiting lists and those that are overdue will be chased regularly.

In a similar way, a statement is required reflecting the handling of interlibrary loans. The second statement may be inappropriate in an LIS that operates primarily by obtaining materials on demand rather than by maintaining its own large stock of documents.

Interlibrary loan requests will be processed within two working days of receipt. Specified deadlines will be met and all requests not supplied within ten working days will be reviewed. Customers will be kept informed of the progress of requests. The LIS will use its best endeavours but cannot influence the lending or copying policies, or the speed of service, of other libraries.

A target of 85% of loans will be satisfied from the LIS's internal stock.

Other services

The following sections contain typical statements relating to the standards for other services.

Online searching

If requested, online searches will be carried out within one working day of receiving the request; otherwise searches are carried out and the results supplied within three working days. If the search is needed urgently, every effort will be made to meet the deadline. If more time is necessary, then a timetable will be agreed with the enquirer.

Printouts from the following databases will be provided on the same day unless agreed otherwise: [list services here].

Printouts from the following databases will be provided within one week unless agreed otherwise, especially if needed more urgently: [list services here; this group is intended for use when offline printing is significantly cheaper than the cost of printing the same information online].

Photocopies

Photocopies from the LIS's stock will be supplied within five working days when the item is not on circulation or loan. Any deadline shorter than this will be met by agreement. Copyright restrictions on the supply of this material will be observed.

The LIS will endeavour to obtain 85% of photocopies from external sources within seven working days. Every effort will be made to meet deadlines. Customers will be kept informed of the progress of their request.

Materials for retention and journals on circulation

Ninety per cent of retention requests will be passed to the acquisitions section for ordering within one working day, the rest within three working days, or they will be passed back to the requester within the same timescale.

Where delivery is not possible within six months (e.g. because of delayed publication of a new title, or heavy demand for a scarce publication), the LIS will consult the issuer of the request to determine what further action should be taken.

The terms above reflect closely those of other paragraphs, but it is important to show the terms that apply to each service, even at the expense of repetition.

Periodicals supplied on subscription will normally be supplied for a minimum of one calendar year. Before renewal instructions are issued, the LIS will issue a notice to registered users of the periodical to judge the likely future demand. Refunds of subscriptions are not normally available after annual renewal. The LIS reserves the right to cancel a subscription if there is insufficient demand or if insufficient users respond to an enquiry.

All periodical parts received by the LIS will be checked-in and circulated within one working day of receipt for items published at monthly intervals or more frequently, or two working days for other materials. Queries will be passed to the acquisitions assistant librarian and will be resolved within two weeks or as soon as the supplier replies.

Reading lists and bibliographical checking

Advice and a bibliographical service will be provided for departments in the organization requiring assistance with book lists.

Reading lists will be produced for departments from LIS's own and external resources as requested and within an agreed timetable.

Database quality management

Controls and procedures will be established, applied and monitored to ensure that all records on the internally created databases that are made available to customers meet minimum standards of quality, including accuracy and completeness.

Housekeeping standards of service

The LIS will maintain a pleasant and safe working environment. The LIS will be tidied daily and LIS staff will ensure that cleaning takes place as scheduled. Areas will be maintained for reading and working with documents. The maintenance department will be contacted about shortcomings, faults and any other matters as necessary.

LIS materials will be reshelved daily and readers' tables cleared daily. Display racks and noticeboards will be checked regularly to remove out-of-date material.

Journals will normally be scanned for the database within three working days, except weekly journals, which will be normally scanned within one working day.

Accurate statistics will be provided within the timetable agreed.

Stock will be kept in good order and in a satisfactory condition. Loose-leaf publications will be regularly updated.

Reading lists will be updated as new publications arrive. These lists will be displayed in the LIS where space allows.

Summary

We hope that the above has helped you to see how important it is to spell out and keep updating the details in your SLA. You will, of course have extra information for your own SLA and we have indicated some further areas of concentration for libraries in different sectors. Remember that only by adhering to the agreement levels will you be able to keep your services cost-effective and efficient. The initial agreement should therefore reflect an attainable, if stretchable target, or liaison with the organization will be restricted to a regular session of explanations and excuses. This is hardly a useful relationship for either party.

Points on which to reflect

- Can you describe the format outline of the SLA document?
- Do you have other available LIS services that you need to include in your SLA?
- Can you describe your service's availability and modes of delivery?

5

Service monitoring

In this chapter we examine:

- **possible requirements for service monitoring**
- **useful and less useful information for inclusion**
- **forms of presentation of monitoring reports**
- **service failures**
- **staff competencies**
- **management uses of service monitoring information**
- **the contract manager's and the LIS manager's viewpoints.**

Where the LIS's SLA is written in response to a tender document or specification, there may be less choice than could be wished in terms of the service monitoring that is to be carried out and reported upon. For example, the Audit Commission's requirement for UK local government LIS authorities to make annual reports on a number of measures from 1998[1] dictates a number of service elements that must be monitored in future.

However, reporting is an essential activity from the standpoint of both parties to the SLA and it is in the LIS manager's interests that it should be undertaken diligently. Among the roles that service monitoring and reporting play are:

- to demonstrate that the LIS is providing the level of service called for by the agreement – this includes LIS staff competencies and updating of LIS staff

- to provide the basis of discussion for liaison meetings between supplier and contract management teams
- to provide a basis for quality control by the supplier as a tool in the management of booksellers or other external suppliers of the LIS
- to act as a basis for renegotiations of charges, service levels, or other elements of the agreement in the light of usage levels.

In addition, where the agreement or tender document contains statements calling for an improvement in efficiency or uptake in the use of the LIS, monitoring will provide information over time to support the claim that this is taking place.

Contents of monitoring reports

Appendix 2 contains a sample format for a regular report or set of reports. However, the tender documents for a service may well include a number of targets for service quality (e.g. 95% of quick reference enquiries to be answered within one hour of receipt) and there is clearly a requirement for responses to such exact targets to be included. A tabular or graphic format is ideal for conveying this information quickly to the reader.

The straightforward presentation of numbers is certainly sufficient to demonstrate the efficient performance of the contract or agreement, but it is of little further value.[2] In particular when there is an obligation to collect such information, the LIS management will gain greater value through the construction of ratios and of time series. Too often, the LIS manager is faced with the problem of working within a hard ('crunchy') accounting regime, which finds it difficult if not impossible to accommodate an LIS whose benefits to the organization are soft ('squashy'). There are issues here that lie beyond the scope of this volume, of quantifying the value of LIS in a way that can be shown on a balance sheet.[3]

Moving beyond simple counting perhaps makes it possible to determine the percentage of photocopy requests from particular journals that are met within the target, or for a particular section of the organization, perhaps thus pointing, for example, to additional subscription requirements or the need to use fax delivery in place of messenger services. A time series will show the LIS's ability to meet a requirement over the course of the year or years, suggesting which sections need reinforcement at holiday times, or for predictable events such as board or council meetings, or the beginning of the fiscal year.

The comparison of quarterly or monthly figures will show trends in the LIS's response to its clients and highlight declining performance before it becomes an issue for dispute with the customer. Measuring quality by surveys will illustrate the reasons behind changes in simple headcounts of those entering the LIS and making enquiries or borrowing books.

Some requests for information contained in service specifications are difficult to meet and may have been included mainly to meet the contract management team's feeling that some kind of 'crunchy' statistics are needed. Thus, one specification might contain a request for both the number of items photocopied and the number of pages copied. While this allows an average number of pages per item copied to be calculated, this figure is of little value. In a research LIS, it would be surprising to find that people were researching consistently from one-column newspaper articles or other current news items; and also, unless there is to be some sort of editorial control over the number of pages requested in any article, there is little that can be done with the information. A comment that the average length per article requested has increased by 0.23 of a page since the last quarter allows neither the LIS manager nor the contract manager to take any meaningful action (beyond, perhaps, ordering an additional box of photocopy paper).

Information retained by the LIS management

The LIS manager needs to decide whether to share with the customer the management information collected, or whether to regard it as internal data. If the information itself is not declared, it may still be a useful technique to include a comment in the report showing that the LIS managers have been observing performance, and have taken steps to correct any developing deficiencies. Where the SLA calls for a commentary on remedial action to deal with faults, it is useful to be able to show that previous monitoring has taken place; access to such information may highlight a new trend, which can be tackled before any management reports are due.

It may be possible to negotiate the exclusion of management information from the customer specification when it would be wasteful or onerous to collect it. In particular, where the tender is drawn up by non-LIS staff, there will probably be elements that appear logical to an accountant or administrator but which are more difficult for the LIS professional to provide, or are of little practical use. This is especially true where the document contains few definitions, so that a bald statement of the number of enquiries handled conveys nothing of the complexity or intellectual level of these enquiries. The LIS professional should take care where such data as unit costs are called for, since the resulting figures may be as good as meaningless (which is not to say that they are of no value if they show a useful year-on-year fall!).

Staff

Since the first edition of this book we have had the opportunity to discuss with staff from many types of LIS what should be included in the SLA on staff and their competencies. The customer will expect to be assured of the knowledge and competencies of the staff delivering the services. The content of the monitoring report will contain a regular report of the continuous professional development of staff.

In Chapter 11 we expand on managing LIS staff, but offer the following for consideration in defining the requirements for this area of the report. Think of all the steps in the process of delivering the services to your customers. LIS staff should have access to the best available tertiary training and education, allowing them to acquire new competencies made necessary by the introduction or advent of new specialist activities, as well as to maintain or improve existing skills for the purpose of career development.

The European Council of Information Associations in their publication *Euroguide LIS – the guide to competencies for the European professional in Library and Information Services*[4] advise that there are four levels of education objectives:

- *Level 1*: Awareness
- *Level 2*: Knowledge of practice or techniques
- *Level 3*: Effective use of the tools
- *Level 4*: Effective use of methodologies.[4]

Aptitudes and attitudes

Generally it is necessary to succeed in developing correct aptitudes and attitudes in staff. Delivering successful information services is dependent on the attitudes of the LIS staff and their ability to be able to perform tasks assigned to them. Rather than having to correct problems, it is better for staff to understand what are the objectives of the services. Monitoring services often reveals lack of training of staff to be able to do the job effectively and efficiently. Therefore staff should be encouraged to ask for appropriate training to acquire the skills needed to do the job in hand.

This is why some indication of the successes and development in competencies of staff should be included in the monitoring report.

Words or figures

A report should not in any case consist of purely statistical information, even if this is what the contract manager ideally wants. As suggested above, information services are too complex to be reduced to a simple list of numbers compared with targets in the manner of a railway reporting on its punctuality. LIS statistics should be accompanied by text that interprets them. Proficiency with spreadsheet software should allow the report to be illustrated not only with tables of statistics but also with graphical representation of the figures. Where the agreement calls for the presentation of information such as an expenditure profile, it is far clearer to offer a table with an accompanying graph than any other form of presentation.

The report should include sections consisting entirely of well written text that conveys progress and achievements. It may include an account of complaints and congratulations, an essay on blue sky topics setting out imminent and longer-term changes, or a description of developing new initiatives. Where increased efficiency in the use of resources has taken place during the reporting period, a point should be made of highlighting this.

It may be helpful to bring out broad trends in the use of the LIS, such as the acceleration of the movement to the use of electronic services as a first resort. Such trends may be easier to present as text commentary than as statistics.

Style

The style and content of the report should be well judged. A very formal style is probably not called for, but it should still be businesslike. The content should deal with the achievement of objectives and the delivery of required outputs. If a section describing the processes is necessary, the report should make clear why this is included, and attempt to be as clear, grammatical and jargon free as possible. As a general rule, the customer is likely to be far more interested in the achievement of the objectives than in the manner in which they were achieved, just as a good service specification will state the outcome to be achieved without prescribing the method.

Drawing attention to other factors

There may have been a change in the targets or objectives, in which case performance figures across the date of the change will not be comparable. This should be highlighted in the report to the contract management team and also taken into account in the LIS's own management processes.

It may be necessary to draw attention to factors affecting performance, for example industrial disputes affecting the LIS or its suppliers, the loss of key members of staff, or the failure of IT networks. Draw attention to those areas that lie outside the LIS's control, particularly where these were noted in the text of the SLA.

Information might be included confirming policies on equal opportunities or the employment of professional staff, noting any relevant ratios. Training policies (such as a commitment to achieve Investors in People status at an agreed future date) might be repeated in each report to demonstrate both commitment and progress in these areas. Adherence to codes of conduct might also be confirmed in the text of the monitoring report.

Frequency

The frequency of the report should be carefully considered. Again, the customer's proposed agreement may lay down a required frequency and the LIS manager may well be content to agree. However, a report at longer than, say, quarterly intervals may make it difficult to indicate emerging difficulties or – rather more positively – to obtain credit for objectives that have been signed off as completed. In particular, when payment depends on completion, frequent and regular reports are necessary.

Service failure

Many SLAs in the field of computing include definitions of service failure and statements of procedures to be followed in this event. Agreements for LIS services can usefully include some of these elements, even if not called upon to do so. It will at least prevent a full-scale emergency being called because the display screen on one terminal is broken, or because a branch librarian has been held up on the way to open the LIS by a railway breakdown.

A definition of service failure is required. The SLA may set out immediate procedures to be followed in the event of failure, and also give details of remedial action, or punitive action in the case of persistent or long-term failure. The examples in the previous paragraph are of the kind that happen readily in normal business and it is to cover these that the wording should be adapted. Branch librarians fall sick while their support staff are on holiday rather more often than entire libraries are flooded or catch fire; but these things happen too, and the emphasis in each case is on the ability to provide an acceptable alternative service in the specified time.

Service failure procedures

Here we suggest some possible wording and definitions. Other definitions of levels of severity than those given here can of course be used. Some organizations, for example, use a range from Level 1 (service failure with an impact that prevents the company's business from operating normally) to Level 4 (minor inconvenience). It may also be worth including a clause in this section to reiterate those situations beyond the LIS's control (discussed in Chapter 3), when service would be suspended, so that it is clear that terms relating to service failure are suspended for the duration of any organization-wide emergency.

---

1   Service failure shall be deemed to be the inability to provide the services required or the inability to provide them to the standards specified in this document, as set out in points 3 to 5. In addition, service failure will be considered to have occurred should any major performance indicator be shown in the end of year report to exceed the variance stated in point 11 below.

2   Service delivery failures will be rectified as soon as possible and in any case within the timescale set out in points 3 to 5 below.

3   Critical service delivery failure means the complete loss of service in one or more locations or any problem otherwise preventing customers from effective use of the LIS for longer than 15 minutes. An initial response will be given to any enquiries from the contract manager within five minutes, and the problem will be resolved by the restoration of the service or the supply of an alternative service within one hour.

4   Major service delivery failure means the partial loss of service in one

location or any problem that will prevent customers from the effective use of any part of the LIS for longer than one hour. An initial response will be given to any enquiries from the contract manager within 15 minutes and the problem will be resolved by the restoration of the service or the supply of an alternative service within four hours.

5   Minor service delivery failure means any other failure of the system or closure of any part of the LIS that prevents efficient use. An initial response will be given to any enquiries from the contract manager within four hours and the problem will be resolved by the restoration of service or the supply of an alternative service within 48 hours.

6   A statement from the LIS management explaining any delay outside their control and agreed by the contract manager shall be considered to be a complete reply to a report of service failure.

7   Nothing in this section shall override the stated requirements of notice to the LIS for any changes required by users. The failure to comply with a demand for service by any user at a new location before the notice has expired shall not be considered as a service failure.

8   If the monitoring of service failures identifies a failure on the part of the supplier to meet the required level of service, then the supplier will prepare, within one month of notice, a statement outlining the methods by which the service will be improved in order to meet the service targets in future. Service will be restored to the required level before the time of the next scheduled service report.

9   The supplier will report to the client on progress at weekly intervals during the implementation of such a plan.

10   If service failures highlight consistent failure by a third-party supplier to meet service requirements, the LIS manager will prepare a report to the contract manager recommending any changes of supplier, the use of penalty clauses, or other action to be taken to restore service.

11   Service performance failure shall be considered to have taken place if any major performance indicator [list] varies from target by more

than the tolerances listed in points 12 to 14 below.

12   Service performance failure shall be considered to have taken place if in any financial year more than one of the performance indicators listed is more than 5% below target without prior agreement.

13   Service performance failure shall be considered to have taken place if in any financial year the supplier fails without prior agreement to achieve in excess of 80% of targets at all quarterly reports.

14   Service performance failure shall be considered to have taken place if in any financial year the number of complaints received from users exceeds 0.01% of the total number of transactions taking place in the LIS.

Acting on the reports

We look more closely at the means of handling complaints in Chapter 7, including the 'escalation' of an unresolved problem; that is, referring it higher up a predefined and agreed management chain on both client and supplier sides until agreement is reached. Let us now look at the management questions that are raised by these reports, and in particular by problems.

Adverse reports, reflecting dissatisfaction by the customer and possibly by the supplier too, can have a number of causes. Most of them can be analysed and resolved within the framework of the SLA process.

Dissatisfaction with the service can be caused by problems to do with the specification. When it has not been prepared by a team with a knowledge of LIS work, there can be elements that are unrealistic and troublesome in practice. Professional input to the specification can help to overcome this, and the LIS team, as the service supplier, should certainly not feel inhibited about proposing change control to overcome poorly specified services. At the same time, there are areas where reasonable expectations on the client's part are not met by the service available to the LIS from external suppliers; here the LIS must act as the client's spokesman in proposing an improvement in service. The introduction of SLAs places a considerable obligation on the LIS to educate its customers about the possible, the difficult and the impossible.[5]

Settling-in period

In the early days of the agreement there is likely to be a settling-in period during which both sides will be coming to terms with the new ways of doing business. Regular meetings are an essential part of this process and should be scheduled frequently. The client will need to be reassured that newly perceived shortcomings are not signs of imminent service failure. The likelihood is that little has changed from the previous ways of business, but that the SLA will have drawn attention to areas of concern for the first time and raised the expectations of a standard of service where perhaps none existed before. There may also be a problem within the LIS if staff members feel that their status has changed and they are less valued than before. They may no longer feel that they belong to the organization in the same way. It is good not only for the LIS as the supplier to be seen to be acting to meet the client's needs but also, if possible, for the client to be flexible in demands in order to reassure the LIS staff. Senior management is best placed to ensure that this happens.

Recurring problems and actions needed

Elements that constantly recur in problem reports clearly need to be acted upon, but change control is an acceptable alternative to remedial action. If the delivery of weekly journals (such as *The Economist*) on a Thursday afternoon is impossible outside central London, the sensible course for an outlying LIS in, for example, Milton Keynes, is to amend its agreement to allow delivery on Friday morning, not to send a member of staff to London by train each week in order to meet contract terms. It is often perfectly possible to meet unreasonable conditions, but it is neither reasonable nor sensible to do so on a regular basis without having overwhelming management reasons.

The process of acting upon the reports – and indeed that of service monitoring overall – comes down to two elements. One is visible cooperation between client and supplier sides, which promotes goodwill. The other is to keep in mind that the ultimate aim is the delivery of an outcome, namely an effective LIS that meets the expressed needs of its users. The performance of LIS processes is only secondary, and those processes may have to be changed if the required outcome is only occasionally achieved in practice.

Summary

We have seen in this chapter that a range of information needs to be drawn out and monitored as the agreement goes into action. The exact content of reports and their frequency will need to be agreed during the negotiation of the agreement.

You need to consider some questions that arise such as:

- What does this information tell me?
- How can it be shared with the customers?
- What needs to be done (by one or more parties to the agreement) to make sure that the information provided by the monitoring exercise is put to good purpose?

6

CHARGING FOR SERVICES

In this chapter we examine:

- how to include information about charges in an SLA
- some ways in which charges are calculated for LIS services
- elements typically included and excluded.

Background

In many organizations, the LIS will be expected to charge out all or part of its service to users. There are a number of useful titles on the costing and charging of LIS services and it is not our intention to explore the underlying issues here.

The LIS has choices in this area that need to be determined at the time of creating the SLA. These range from the keeping of detailed records of the inputs to each piece of work and charging for the resources actually consumed, to maintaining a comprehensive tariff and issuing invoices according to the number of units of work consumed over a given period.

In between come approaches that provide a mixture, for example charging a set sum for loans or interlibrary loans, while providing research services on a time and materials basis.

Variations on the extremes include the precalculation of charges based on previous volumes of use and the issue of a lump-sum invoice at the outset of an accounting period.

In each case, the introduction of charges for what is commonly seen as a free good has serious implications for the management of the LIS that is using SLAs.

Information about LIS charges

An SLA will frequently need to include information about the charges to be made for information and LIS services. There are a number of different approaches to setting out the charges; we examine these below.

Detailed information about charges should be excluded from the main document. If it is made a part of the wording of the body of the SLA, change control will have to be invoked each time there is some adjustment to the prices. This is an ineffective way of working and makes unnecessary administrative work. The proper place is in a schedule or annexe to the document where the tariff or other list can be set out. The body of the agreement should include a reference such as:

> The charges for the information service as set out in Annexe X are agreed and will be paid by means of a transfer of funds once every three months on the first working day of June, September, December and March. The charges in Annexe X may be varied by agreement not less than four weeks in advance of the next due payment date.

Types of charges

In setting up an LIS under an SLA including costing and charging, decisions must be made about two elements of the financial regime: first, whether to adopt a form of cost recovery scheme; and second, the basis on which any such scheme will operate.

LIS have traditionally been seen as a free service, whatever the true cost of providing it. Indeed, much of the professional ethic of librarians is founded on this assumption. A result is an ingrained reluctance to charge users for services, and a tendency to underestimate their true cost. However, LIS are increasingly faced with the need to introduce a charging regime, so the first of these decisions may well be dictated by the corporate environment of the LIS. The focus is then on the second question, with decisions to be made about means of maximizing the use of the service.

The maintenance of high levels of use will keep down the unit cost of transactions, and thus make the LIS tariff more attractive to users. Low cost may well attract use, although (as we discuss later in the section on customer responsibilities) the LIS may be able to insist on a clause in the SLA binding customers to it as the first port of call for information requests for part or all of the SLA's duration, thus allowing it to set a tariff in the knowledge that it will not be undercut by an external predator, which may raise its own tariffs once the internal LIS has been put out of business by price undercutting.

Where a charged-for service is established, charges may be calculated and the costs of the LIS may be accounted for in a number of ways:

- full cost recovery[1]
- partial recovery, with a central service being provided by the core organization and users meeting the identifiable direct costs of services such as online searches or interlibrary loans
- flat-rate subscriptions.

There are many shades between these models, particularly where some, but not all, overheads are added to direct costs.[2] The charges levied within these options also give scope for a variety of approaches. They can be calculated as, for example: input based (e.g. hourly charges for time spent and fully accounted for); average rates for tasks performed, with some measure of assessment of complexity providing a broadly stepped tariff based on preset scales; and tariffs that ignore the time spent on each enquiry.

The user should ideally be given a choice of these types of charges, but it may be necessary to direct this choice, for example if the organization favours a particular accounting style. There may be reasons why one of these types is unsuitable, perhaps because the average cost of an operation is high and appears unjustifiable. For example, 'If the cost of a loan is £20, why not give the department £10 to buy a copy of their own? That way they obtain a copy to keep and the LIS saves £10.'

All the options above, except the subscription approach, involve the LIS in detailed record keeping. While the LIS may already keep records, there is an overhead, particularly when the names of customer departments and of the individual members of their staff have to be recorded. The final cost of running a detailed charging regime may be high.

The subscription option is crude, but has the advantage that the LIS can calculate its available funds at the start of the year. If a department buys a subscription but then makes poor use of it, the LIS does not suffer.

However they are finally determined, it is important that charges:

- are understood and accepted by the user
- are reported to the user at regular and frequent intervals
- are consistent: if there are variations between customers, this must be explained and agreed (e.g. discounts for a guaranteed level of enquiry work or surcharges for work above an agreed ceiling limit)
- are simple to account and charge for
- allow ready comparison with other providers or suppliers
- reflect the level of service and are adjusted accordingly if the service level changes
- can be renegotiated to the satisfaction of both the LIS and the customer if either party's funds are liable to run out, leading to the possibility of breach of the agreement.

What the SLA charges include

The SLA needs to make clear what is included in the charges. LIS do not just provide information services in a vacuum; they provide, or rather share, their allocation of accommodation, heat, light, power, telephones and other corporate services. If the LIS were not there, a certain proportion of these facilities would not be needed by the organization. It is therefore reasonable to add a charge representing the user's proportion of the additional costs to the organization's facilities management of having an LIS. Changes in public sector accounting are under way that will make it important to be familiar with all of these elements, just as those in the private sector have to be already.

It would be a very harsh financial regime that felt justified in adding charges for lighting or heating the LIS to an enquirer's bill; although it is arguably desirable to include the costs such as telephone calls made in order to connect to online databases.

A notional cost of accommodation for a book issued on loan is, again, possibly a reasonable surcharge. A book kept in an office in central London may well cost £5 a year to store, taking into account the unused space around it. If it is issued twice a year, should the LIS absorb or pass on the £2.50 element of storage costs to each user, or should LIS book selection policy be so accurate that it is not worth collecting the cost of storage for a book that is hardly ever in the LIS anyway?

A further question relevant to organizations that operate a full-cost accounting system is to determine the depreciation in value of bookstock. It may be argued that the value of many books should be written off only over a period of many years; but it is far harder to contend that the cost of annual reference books should be allocated to more than one year. This is a question over which long philosophical arguments could be raised, probably to no useful purpose. The main thing is to agree some method with the company accountants that either considers the stock to have no monetary value (which is the simplest solution) or adopts an easy formula to allocate a notional life to the LIS stock, which can then be written off over an agreed period.

This part of the SLA should ideally include a statement of ownership of the stock. It will normally be the case that the client owns the stock rather than the LIS as a separate entity, but even this raises other questions. To avoid future dispute, statements should be included setting out ownership and allocating the power to dispose of surplus stock and to take other management action.

XYZ Co. retains title at all times to the published and unpublished stock contained in the XYZ LIS and to all new materials added. XYZ Co. shall

at all times be considered the legal owner of the LIS stock, except that the LIS staff of XYZ LIS may dispose of outdated, damaged and otherwise unwanted stock in the course of their business.

Where an item is valued at over £50 at the time of disposal, the librarian shall request permission from the client side agreement manager for its disposal. No items shall be disposed of to the second-hand book trade unless all ownership markings have been obliterated. Any monies accruing from the sale of unwanted publications shall be paid to central funds, but the librarian may request an additional allocation of bookfund monies equal to the amounts credited.

Expenses incurred by the LIS

Does the LIS have to make contributions to services which, in turn, do not make use of the LIS? Should these costs be included in the LIS charges? Examples include:

- messenger services
- reception desk
- catering
- personnel management
- welfare services.

The last two, together with other corporate services such as health and safety, should ideally be your customers!

It may be necessary to spell out other details, such as funding for new media developments, since it is difficult to forecast new LIS-based activities five years in the future. Ask pertinent but realistic questions: if your LIS had signed a five-year agreement for services and IT support in 1993, who would have paid for the equipment to access the internet, and how would that have been charged back?

Reporting

As we saw earlier, the SLA should specify that the client receives a report at monthly or other specific intervals setting out the LIS's performance in the previous period. The report should include any specified numerical data, together with the charges for services, where these are levied. Not all of the report will be suitable for simple enumeration; textual commentary will need to be added.

Charges should be set to give the users a choice of options in paying for the service. Where the service varies up or down in quantity or quality, the charges should follow suit. This should make it simple to compare costs between suppliers.

Service charges and other elements of an SLA

Further responsibilities may be set out in the SLA. These may be charged for, or otherwise absorbed as part of the overheads of the LIS. Where a charge is to be included in the agreement for the services listed below, some kind of estimate is needed of the effort that will go into their performance. Account must be taken of the level of seniority at which each task will be managed and/or carried out. For tasks that are carried out occasionally, it may be more useful to have a 'consultancy' tariff (for example, pricing the chief librarian's time at £450 a day to include all overheads) and to apply this rather than attempting to cost all elements of a staff member's time in arriving at a price for each case.

Management of complaints

Escalation procedures need to be carefully set out:

All complaints received by XYZ LIS from customers will be logged and investigated. Valid complaints regarding the provision of services will be separately identified and recorded.

All complaints will receive an official response from the Manager of XYZ LIS or an authorized deputy within two weeks of receipt, and where further investigation is needed, a full response within five weeks.

Where the user is not satisfied by such a response to a complaint, he or she may refer it to the secretary of the LIS user committee.

The register of complaints will be available to members of the LIS user committee on request and to all other users by agreement with the LIS contract manager.

Representational duties

Under an SLA, it is useful to include specific agreement and authority for members of the LIS to attend professional meetings, etc., and to identify themselves as speaking on behalf of the employing organization.

XYZ LIS will represent the interests of XYZ, and attend meetings or provide advice and guidance as appropriate, being identified as authorized representatives of the organization.

Representation may well extend as far as providing a public voice for the organization. Surveys often highlight the public relations role of libraries, providing a safe conduit for communication with other organizations initially on a LIS-to-LIS basis before the responsible parties in the two bodies are put in touch with each other on the question in hand. Where the LIS is operating on a contractual basis it is as well to include a suitable reference that not only permits this behaviour but also acknowledges its value.

XYZ LIS will deal with initial enquiries from the public and other organizations, and forward bona fide requests from other commercial bodies to the appropriate liaison officer.

When the LIS takes enquiries other than by telephone it may be useful to provide a list of the methods used and response times.

XYZ LIS will handle general information enquiries received by the organization and delivered or redirected to LIS as follows: [for example]

- telephone: within 24 hours (urgent in 60 minutes), reply by telephone or memorandum/letter as appropriate
- in person: as for telephone
- written: within one week, reply by post
- fax: within 48 hours, reply by fax
- electronic mail: within 48 hours, reply by electronic mail unless printed items are being sent, when one week by post.

Advice, guidance and professional work

It is easy to underestimate the amount of advice and guidance that a LIS may give, not only in its traditional skill areas, but also in new areas such as the internet and even the use of word-processing packages. This heading allows a commitment by both parties to maintaining the levels of knowledge and professional expertise required to meet this obligation. A statement should also be included about standards, as well as any disclaimers. If the norm in the organization is not to double-check or triple-check information, the customer's attention must be drawn to the level of confidence in the data used, and any additional costs for such reliability must be indicated. Alternatively, some users, such as senior management personnel, might be offered a premium service within their subscription and others given access to this at an additional fee.

XYZ LIS will provide services of a high standard, and will ensure that all internally generated information is indexed and maintained professionally. In particular, databases will be subject to quality checking.

XYZ LIS will endeavour to use external databases of similar standing, but cannot guarantee 100% accuracy of this information. Customers should identity those requests where the normal level of reliability is insufficient and where absolute verification is required. Further charges for additional database searches are by arrangement, unless the user has subscribed to the premium information service in which case this level of accuracy is already assured.

XYZ LIS will maintain the professional skills of its staff at a sufficient level to maintain these standards, subject to the continuing availability of the agreed training funds.

Training

Many LIS will need to become involved in training end-users to take full advantage of the LIS, its facilities and other information-relevant software. An SLA should set out this commitment, preferably including a note of the workload involved.

XYZ LIS should be involved in the provision of training courses to teach good practice in information use, particularly internal databases, CD-ROMs, the internet and the intranet. The manager of training services should consult the manager of the LIS to ensure proper involvement in these and in induction courses for the staff of XYZ.

XYZ LIS will meet the same quality standards in providing such courses as those adopted by training services.

XYZ LIS will ensure that written instructions included in its procedures manual and used as a training aid are kept up to date. Each section will be updated at least six-monthly to take account of revised procedures in the LIS.

There may be a requirement to establish procedures manuals and other documentation, if this does not already exist. In the controlled environment of service level management it is often necessary to document procedures that are well known by everyone and have operated without written instructions for a long time.

It is the need to account for operations to a third party outside the LIS that makes this documentation necessary. This gives a useful opportunity to ensure that there are not more obviously efficient ways of achieving the same ends and outputs before laboriously documenting an outmoded procedure.

The creation of manuals from scratch is an arduous business and the time taken to do this should not be underestimated. For this and for many other reasons, it is useful for an LIS team to negotiate for the first report on service to be delivered at the end of the second (and not the first) quarter of operation.

Financial and accounting controls

The LIS should be committed to maintaining proper financial and audit controls, especially where its service is being provided by a team that includes external contractors or where the controls of the parent body could be argued no longer to apply to a team effectively being held at arm's length from the organization.

Central government accounting is now broadly in line with private sector practice and the system known as Resource Accounting and Budgeting (RAB) in government has produced a number of changes to previous practice. Many agencies and other public sector bodies already use accounting systems of this type. You may wish to include a clause in the SLA which draws attention to the accounting system that is used, particularly where differing systems are used by the organizations involved in a partnership, or where the partners have different accounting years.

The financial and accounting procedures of XYZ shall be applied at all times in the management of XYZ LIS. The fiscal year shall be from 1 April

to 31 March in the following calendar year and the managers of XYZ LIS shall prepare financial reports at the end of each quarter in line with the financial management handbook. The managers and staff of XYZ LIS as employees of XYZ shall be fully accountable for compliance with this code, and contract staff must accept this accountability as a condition of employment.

Sums of money received by the LIS must be accounted for in line with the financial management handbook and will be credited to central accounts received. They may not be directly used by the LIS without the written agreement of the director of finance.

IT issues

Finally, the LIS needs to look at a number of IT-related issues, such as the supply of LIS-specific information technology services and access to internet-delivered information services. In an organization that is contracting out support services and managing those that it retains in-house by SLA, there may be difficulties in handling LIS-related IT.

LIS IT is widely believed by both librarians and IT professionals to be more difficult to install, manage and operate than mainstream office system applications. Add to the problems of LIS management systems those of electronic mail (including links to the internet and the possible need to introduce firewalls not required by other parts of the organization) and the telecommunications issues connected with online searching and the internet, and the result is that libraries often choose to retain control of their information technology in-house, as an alternative to spending time handholding support teams from an IT supplier.

However, this, like everything else, needs stating in an SLA. It is necessary to list hardware and software that is supported by the LIS, and to spell out which parts of the system are supported by the organization's IT section (such as, probably, the connection to the office automation system providing networked word-processing and internal electronic mail).

This is probably one of the most tedious sections of the SLA, consisting of references to an annexe listing serial numbers of personal computers and software packages (putting this information in the main agreement would be a considerable problem in terms of change control), but it is also one of the most important, for it establishes exactly what equipment the LIS must look after itself and what the organization must, if necessary, mend to the LIS's satisfaction.

It is important to remember to include LIS-specific elements of the network (such as TCP/IP protocols) if these are likely to conflict with the organization's network, and make it entirely clear who is responsible for resolving any system conflicts arising from their presence on a network whose users do not otherwise need them.

Web-based information services

The development of a range of information services available over the internet complicates matters somewhat. Since the first edition of this book, it has become common for members of large organizations to have access to these services from their desktop or for copies of the databases in question to be loaded on to an intranet for local use. In the first instance, the SLA needs to reflect the position of the LIS: is the supplier contract managed by the LIS on behalf of the organization, or are there in effect a number of separate concurrent contracts, of which only one is for library use? In the second example, the SLA will need to make it clear where responsibilities divide: who is responsible for the currency of the database, and who for the continuing technical support that ensures connection to the internet? This latter issue needs particularly clear definition. Finally, you may want to include a condition that allows you to gather information to be used in calculating your own charges.

The LIS will be responsible for maintaining current subscriptions to the third-party information services listed in Annexe K of this agreement. It will manage negotiations with the suppliers to ensure that best value is obtained for all such subscriptions.

The [Technical Support Section] of XYZ Ltd will support end-users in resolving technical issues concerning the operation of the browser software used to access the third-party information services. The LIS will provide support and training in the use of the databases and the information contained in them, including searching, sorting and printing records. All problems will be referred to the [Technical Support Section] Help Desk in the first instance, who will contact LIS if the problem relates to information use and management. LIS will refer users reporting technical problems to the [Technical Support Section] and will retain only problems relating to the use of the information content of the databases supplied.

LIS will pass any relevant technical information supplied by third-party information service suppliers to the [Technical Support Section] for information and to support their planning.

[Technical Support Section] will provide LIS with details of the chargeable search sessions carried out by [names of individuals, names of sections or departments] within 00 days of the end of each calendar month, to permit the LIS to calculate the sums to be recharged to users. This information will include, as a minimum, the User name, User ID, time and date of the session, databases used, duration of connection, and summary of charges transmitted from the database host.

A review meeting will take place at least every month in order to consider problems with third-party information services reported during the previous period, and to agree any remedial action needed such as improved publicity concerning changes, additional training, etc.

Summary

This chapter has focused on a number of concerns around charging and other financial questions that you are likely to have to cover in your SLA. You need to think through the special factors that apply in your library and information service, and decide how to deal with these in the agreement:

- What will you be charging for, now or – if you can reliably forecast – in the initial period of the SLA?
- What is the financial regime that you need to operate within? Are there any consequent issues because of the systems used by your partners and suppliers? What conditions do you need to put on contractors or suppliers?
- Whom are you dependent upon internally? What must you do to ensure that you receive sufficient information to protect your own financial interests, and to ensure that lines of demarcation are sufficiently clear to free you from any concerns over costs incurred for services outside your control?

7
MANAGING YOUR CUSTOMERS

In this chapter we examine the importance of relationships with your customers:

- when the SLA is being negotiated
- when you want the customer to sign the agreement
- in persuading the customer to accept certain responsibilities
- in monitoring the service
- in case of problems
- where third-party suppliers are involved.

Introduction

Why should the service level manager need to manage the customer? The LIS manager must do so partly as a form of customer education (to create the so-called 'intelligent customer'), and partly to avoid problems in service level management. The customer, as one of the parties to the agreement, has expectations and assumptions about the service, which the LIS manager needs to manage (or even manipulate). If there are not to be any unpleasant surprises in operating the SLA, the LIS manager must ensure that the customer understands the service as well as being satisfied with it. This includes understanding what the service does not provide as well as what it does.

Benefits lie both in ensuring the smooth operation of the current agreement and in preparation for changes to the agreement. By the time of its eventual renewal, the customer's understanding of the LIS's business should have improved to the point where real choices can be made and a more satisfactory agreement reached than for each previous period.

What exactly needs to be managed?

- *Demands*: what the customer wants, especially if it falls outside the specification.
- *Expectations*: what the customer thought would be on offer, particularly if these expectations arise from a service specification that was prepared without significant input from the LIS.
- *Perceptions*: the customer's view of what the LIS is delivering (and doing for others) compared with the client's demands and expectations.

It would be easy to be pessimistic about these. There is no escalation procedure for success built into the average SLA. However, this cannot be a one-sided affair. Customers have responsibilities too and the LIS manager can achieve success by managing these.

What the customer wants

Strictly speaking, it is not the supplier's task to define what the customer wants. The LIS manager is asked to agree a specification, and may well negotiate the terms available, but the definition must ultimately be the customer's, and not the supplier's. (This criticism has been levelled particularly at the purchaser–provider relationship in the NHS.)

Suppliers are, however, at liberty to suggest what services they would like to provide. Some do so, for example by issuing model specifications that just happen to match the services that they sell. If services under the agreement can be modified in line with changing need, then the agreement should also spell out the customer's rights and responsibilities, and address the issues of continuing service during negotiation and of the funding for the new services within the financial framework of the SLA.

Customers must feel that they have been fully consulted and that in effect they share the ownership of the service definition that is enshrined in the SLA.[1,2] A focus group approach may work well here, bringing together representatives from different parts of the organization – possibly with differing or even conflicting requirements. They need to consider questions such as these – and agree answers:

- What features are needed in a library and information service for the organization (or in various services for different parts of it)?
- What value does each group attach to it, and what is their perception of its value to the organization as a whole?
- How much monetary value does the group attach to the service, and would they be willing to pay this amount if hard charging were introduced?
- Which services will be a standard part of the LIS offer, and which ones optional (and charged) extras?
- What incentives would the users like to offer the LIS in order to develop services they require?

The LIS manager would be well armed in these negotiations with a copy of a service statement for the LIS that he or she operates. This specification is capable of expansion into the basis of an SLA, and provides users with a clear statement of what is already in the standard service offer. This starting point avoids the need for the customer to invest time and effort in learning the definition of LIS terminology and makes it easier for the client side to develop an 'intelligent customer' function. However care has to be taken to define terminology very carefully. In this situation, the usual confusion between different senses of technical terms needs to be avoided, as does the use of LIS jargon, if disputes are to be avoided. For example, does circulation mean journals circulation or routing, or does it mean monograph circulation or loans? What is 'a hold'? Does the term imply that the item will be physically held until the client collects it, or will the item be sent to the client via internal or external post?

What is obvious to the LIS manager is not necessarily obvious to the client, and needs spelling out in detail. A ready-made glossary such as British Standard 7408 is a starting point, although even this does not resolve the problem of professional jargon that the user does not understand.

Using a service statement or brochures produced by the LIS, the customer's needs can be matched to specific services listed, or it can be explained how a service or combination of services will meet a particular customer need. It is often more useful to discover, as with the reference interview technique, what need the customer is trying to meet when he or she describes a service that they want but which the LIS does not have and does not wish to develop: often, customers describe a process that they believe will deliver the required result, rather than a service they actually need. Once the available services are matched to the customer's requirement, not only is it easier to demonstrate the value of agreeing to use the LIS's services but much of the definition of the SLA has taken place and has been validated by the negotiation process.

Negotiating and agreeing the terms

At the end of this process you need to have arrived at some agreed statement of what the customer wants, couched in the kind of terms that can be passed to potential suppliers on the one hand, and that will satisfy the corporate legal department on the other.

Many LIS staff seem to resent the time spent on the negotiation of the terms of the SLA, saying that they have more urgent use for the time to undertake professional tasks. This negotiation activity, as with time invested in user education, will, however, save time later through the avoidance of disputes. It can be a painstaking and tedious process, especially for early customers. Not only are these customers who cannot be presented with an SLA that is already widely adopted, which they will therefore be hard-put to alter or substantially rewrite, they are also likely to be high-profile corporate users (or they certainly should be). The company lawyers are a useful early signatory, as you can probably rely on their devoting considerable unpaid time to fashioning the SLA to their own satisfaction.

Signing up senior management and other large departments is worthwhile. Starting with smaller customer groups for practice is likely to throw up too many anomalies and may miss the core requirements of the company altogether.

Continual customer education

Customers need to understand that using the LIS properly, as it was intended, e.g. using manuals and guides, is of mutual benefit to both customer and supplier. It follows that the LIS manager must give continual feedback and information to the customer on developments in LIS services. If an external 'expert' was used to prepare it, the service specification is particularly likely to define an LIS that is the affordable balance between cost and feasibility at the date of its preparation. Development in LIS continues at high speed. The world wide web, for example, went from being an interesting sideline to an essential information tool in less than the average life of an LIS contract. The LIS manager must provide users with sufficient knowledge to review the specification whenever necessary, and must encourage this process. It is to no one's advantage for customers to find that a more up-to-date service would have suited them better. The LIS manager will be behind the field, while the customer's reaction to such a discovery may well be to blame the LIS manager for failing to point out the shortfalls.

An hour spent in user education may save several more from being wasted later on in resolving complaints. Frequent presentations may be one way of achieving this, perhaps as part of the liaison meetings where a standard agenda item might be 'service developments and new products'. This would allow not only a presentation of new initiatives from the LIS but also allow the staff to show off promising new products from the information world marketplace to see which are worthwhile pursuing, perhaps with the intention of inviting suppliers to present their products (free of charge, of course) to a future meeting, thus enhancing further the LIS's reputation for being at the leading edge of development.

Customers also need to understand and appreciate the full implications of working within the copyright and other intellectual property laws, and once again time spent in education will be amply repaid through the avoidance of disputes. This becomes more important still where application service providers (ASPs) are employed, since customers may infringe the intellectual property rights of others with whom the contractual arrangement is managed by the LIS. The SLA needs to highlight that in these instances the responsibility is the customer's, and perhaps to state explicitly the terms of indemnification. While this may be somewhat academic where ultimately the legal responsibility falls on a named individual such as the company secretary who is not a member of the LIS or of the offending section, it needs to be clearly stated how far the LIS's liability extends.

Customers should be encouraged to ask for training where necessary, e.g. in the use of computerized services. They also need to understand that the use of passwords to get into these services needs to be managed properly. The LIS will need to ensure that the customer understands the reasons for this, especially important if hard charging is applied. The LIS must ensure that the customer understands the LIS budget and the control mechanisms in place.

This kind of management is especially valuable since the SLA should be couched in terms that demand the customer's loyalty. It is impossible to plan staff and other resource management if the LIS manager is constantly unsure of the likely demand for services.

Providing feedback

A recognized two-way channel for feedback between the supplier and the customer is essential. If there are difficulties, the supplier should not have to guess why an agreement is under threat or a breach alleged, so there needs at least to be a means of channelling complaints and ensuring their resolution. It is worth having a clause insisting that this procedure is exhausted before a breach is signalled. This entails the customer reflecting the structure and procedures of the supplier's organization to the extent of providing a named point of contact, including deputies and escalation procedures.

Engaging the customer in a continuous dialogue can be very helpful in shaping and delivering the type of service they need. Ensuring that the customers' needs are fully understood can be usefully achieved through encouraging feedback, whether good or bad. The process can reinforce messages about their own responsibilities, for example, in alerting the LIS of any changes in their requirements. This could be a new area of work for the customers, changes of direction, new staff needing different levels of information. The 'how', 'why', 'when', 'to whom', and so on should be written into the SLA. (We saw at the end of Chapter 6 that you should also consider the ways in which you draw upon your customers' conversations with related suppliers, such as technical help desks.)

There are further ways in which customer feedback can help the LIS deliver a better service. For example, subject specialists will be able to give the LIS warning of important new publications. Customers can also be 'managed' through a dialogue that encourages them to give the fullest details available for requests and enquiries.

Customer surveys are a sound means of ensuring that feedback is obtained. A quarterly review will give an opportunity to ask specific questions about under- or over-used services, as well as a basket of broader regular enquiries about user satisfaction and requirements. Adding sufficient space for comments, or enquiring about developing requirements in an open question, will provide early warning of fresh needs or emerging difficulties.

Feedback from the customer should also include warnings of unusual workloads, such as those arising from new projects. Normal volumes of work should be defined in the service specification, together, perhaps, with an agreed ceiling for peak loads above which deadlines and costs become negotiable outside the agreement proper. This allows the LIS manager to schedule resources more effectively and to remain within budget while being flexible in meeting the customer's new requirements.

In the other direction, formalized feedback helps the LIS manager by providing a channel for news of success in meeting targets, highlighting potentially useful developments in LIS work, and so forth.

Feedback has one other benefit; it helps to eliminate nasty surprises, which often otherwise occur at contract review meetings. We shall look at the wider issues of keeping in touch with the customer later in this chapter. Suppliers need to be able to plan and be able to deliver the services to schedule and operate profitably or at least within budget, with no nasty surprises for any party.

Managing problems

Sooner or later some kind of problem will occur in the relationship with the customer. We saw above that this may arise because of:

- *demand*: something new, which the customer wants done and the LIS has not been contracted to provide
- *expectation*: something the customer thought would be done but which the LIS does not consider has been specified
- *perception*: something the customer expected to be done but which the LIS did in a different way or at a different time or to a different level.

All problems become worse if they are left to fester. The LIS manager must insist that any perceived shortfalls are reported to the LIS help desk as soon as possible. The help desk has two initial functions at this point, contributing to the aims of both calming and resolving. The first is to ensure that there is a fault or shortfall, so that the LIS can take remedial action. The second is to dissuade the customer from carrying out a do-it-yourself fix on the problem, and possibly making it worse.

Some tact is called for by the help desk staff. The educational function will initially be to the fore, since the answer may be contained in documentation held by the customer, when the solution is the one identified in family publications as 'read the friendly manual'.

Help desk staff also need a flexible approach. No useful purpose is served by those who use the SLA as a fixed statement of the services they are permitted to offer, and refuse to consider how other demands can be met, even against payment. The customer is not pleased to be told what could have been done, if only there were not an SLA in place.

Using the LIS properly

Customers cannot truly complain if the service that they have specified turns out to be inadequate. When this occurs, it may be useful to reinforce messages on the proper use of the LIS and its facilities, to ensure that no customers decide to alter the rules in their favour in an attempt to improve matters. Without such insistence, it may be difficult to operate the LIS within financial or other targets. The answer to such a situation must be to negotiate changes to suit all parties. An 'I told you so' response from LIS staff is unlikely to win new friends but it is reasonable to insist that customers stick to the agreement until the changes are implemented.

This certainly must extend to the use of passwords, LIS pass cards, and similar means of controlling access and costs. 'No card, no service' is a suitably memorable slogan. Another important lesson is that, if you give your access code to someone else, you pay when they use it. The LIS cannot operate in a hard-charging regime if it constantly has to transfer charges between accounts or has to argue about who actually used the service. The LIS must insist on being treated no differently from other parts of the organization in this respect.

If there are local rules relating to levels of authority needed to order publications, copying, printing, etc., these should also appear in the SLA, while the LIS should lose no opportunities to insist that statutory responsibilities under a range of legislation (including intellectual property and freedom of information) lies with the end-user. The LIS may need to agree a common approach with others such as the archives service – and certainly with the legal section.

Telling the customers about their responsibilities

The SLA must specify those tasks that do not form part of your service, but that a customer might expect the LIS to undertake. Some possible examples are:

• updating looseleaf legal publications

- checking receipt of periodicals that are delivered directly to users
- ordering or distributing press copies of the organization's publications
- obtaining afternoon newspapers.

It is as well to compile a list of such issues and check on them from time to time. However you may have time to arrange room clearances that include piles of unopened looseleaf amendments or incomplete journal runs; you may even enjoy doing so.

Similarly, when the customer takes part in an LIS process, for example by inputting to a database, the responsibilities need to be set out. Is there a code or manual that has to be applied in data entry? Must a particular thesaurus or cataloguing code be applied? Whose responsibility is it to edit inadequate entries to meet the standard and who accepts the cost if an entry is rejected by an external buyer of the resulting records?

You will also need to specify some everyday responsibilities, such as telling the LIS when people move offices. More LIS-orientated responsibilities must include rules on such matters as taking responsibility for materials handed to other users without passing back through the LIS, and in particular, taking financial responsibility for lost or overdue materials borrowed from other libraries. Customers must acknowledge that their behaviour in returning borrowed material may affect the entire organization, and that the organization's move to an internal contractual basis does not affect the outside world's perception of it. This clearly extends to issues such as an insistence that only the LIS may place orders with suppliers, and that departments placing any irregular orders must pay the invoice.

Legal constraints

LIS managers and staff are of course used to various legal constraints, but general users are, arguably, not aware of them. The SLA therefore needs to echo (by reference to other documents rather than by exhaustive listing) the requirements affecting the LIS's service. In particular, there should be references to copyright regulations (bearing in mind that librarians may have

privileges not granted to the rest of the organization). It may be worth referring to all the licensing organizations with whom the parent body has
concluded agreements. Other licence agreements should also be referred to,
such as those commonly attached to computer disks and CD-ROMs bound
into books. This may also be a useful place to insert conditions relating to
safeguarding against computer viruses.

Things to prevent

The customer should sign up to a number of specific responsibilities that provide the LIS with some stability and protection, and allow it to plan in the
longer term. This means that the SLA should contain an agreement not to
use the LIS budget for the purchase of other LIS services, such as signing up
to a business reference LIS service. This might extend to departmental use
of online services if agreement can be reached, although end-user searching
is becoming rather too commonplace to resist forever, and this issue is complicated by the arrival of the internet. There needs to be sufficient stability
and protection to allow the LIS to employ its staff confidently for the period
of the agreement. During discussions about such protection, it may become
clearer whether charging a flat rate or operating a per-enquiry tariff offers the
LIS the greater stability.

Difficulties

In an internal financial regime controlled by SLAs, the LIS may find it has
been given blunt teeth to enforce its sanctions. Can delinquent borrowers
really be cut off? Is the LIS in breach of its agreement if it does so? In what
circumstances would the SLA be suspended? Any number of events can close
the LIS, which are outside its control. Should the clock continue to run for
service level measurement while it does so?

A one-hour fire drill will cause an LIS to fail to meet a 98% service target
in an average week's opening. During the exercise, any number of telephone calls will fail a 15-second target to be answered (does an answerphone

message meet it?). The LIS could be affected by power failure, health and safety closures (extreme cold, water damage . . .), equipment failure, etc. If central services, such as power, heating and lighting are supplied by the organization, the LIS's SLA should specify failure of those services as a reason to suspend service measurement.

The agreement could helpfully include definitions of severity levels. Is a problem trivial or does it prevent any work until it is resolved? How soon does it therefore need to be fixed? These levels should be used in completing the help desk logs, which the LIS manager should expect to show regularly to the contract manager. Remember that the time to fix may be more important to one group than another. It may be that you have to adopt different severity levels for the same problem at various times of the day or week in order to reflect priorities realistically.

See also Chapter 5.

Keeping in touch

Regular meetings between the two sides will ensure that many of these issues can be managed easily, although, again, a 'no surprises' regime should be encouraged. Meetings should be frequent enough to allow problems to be resolved before they become difficult to handle. On the other hand, it is useful for them to be sufficiently well spaced to allow comprehensive new reports on service achievements to be presented to each meeting.

These meetings will help to identify key players (and their deputies) from each side and to keep them in personal contact, helping to avoid confrontation. They should be focused on service development and the reporting of successful achievement, rather than on examining shortfalls and failures of service. The help desk logs will provide useful information for these meetings.

Escalation

Escalation procedures should be set out for the resolution of disputes when the original parties cannot agree. Normally, this will be the managers on each side. If resolution is still not achieved, the issue goes a stage further up each managerial line. A final arbiter will then be consulted if no agreement is reached.

In selecting the final arbiter, as we saw in Chapter 2, it is important to consider where the management line from each party finishes. If both paths lead to the same desk, disputes will not be easily resolved. The lines should finish at least one level below the manager in common to both parties; this should be specified to prevent further escalation. It is worth considering how far up the organization there is likely to be any understanding of the issues involved. Will the financial director have anything useful to say to the marketing manager about the replacement value of a lost interlibrary loan? Whoever you choose, the individuals should be named. If one of them moves, change control should be invoked to name the replacement in the agreement, although you could and should reduce this need by specifying the post rather than naming the postholder as far as possible.

Change control

The SLA that casts in stone the LIS of five years ago is of little lasting use. Therefore, a system of change control is required, to allow amendments, deletions and additions to be made to reflect current requirements and resources. Without it, unsatisfactory clauses cannot be changed and a satisfactory contract cannot be extended without a complete re-tendering exercise. The SLA should therefore say what procedures need to be followed and how they (and the agreement reached) are recorded. It should be stated whether changes have to be by mutual consent, or whether one party can agree changes with a third party, such as a management board, and bypass the other party's contract managers.

Other issues

Related issues that we examine in other sections of this book are: managing third parties, and what happens in the case of default.

You rely on many third parties, internally and externally, to deliver your service. These include your own suppliers, such as booksellers and journals agents, your internal messenger service, couriers and the postal authorities. How is your SLA worded in the case where you are failed by one of them? This question is examined more closely in Chapter 9.

You need to be clear about whether the LIS would go on supplying a service in case of default, and if notice had been served to quit. This means that your contracts with others should have a break clause inserted, and that the documents described earlier in this chapter should be kept up to date in case they are needed unexpectedly for a new tender negotiation exercise.

Summary

The section of an SLA that binds the customer to certain behaviours or to specified commitments towards the LIS is usually one of the shortest parts of the agreement, but it is among the most important. In a very real sense, the agreement is not an agreement without it. So it needs to be carefully written. After reading this section you should be considering how the SLA will reflect:

- what the customers' true requirements are, and the ways in which you will discover them
- what behaviour you expect of your customers, both in the way they approach the LIS and in the way that they choose to find information other than by using the LIS
- what steps you will take to ensure that the dialogue is continuing, and does not take place only at the start and end of the period of the agreement
- what education and training your users therefore require in order to understand and meet their obligations.

8
Outsourcing services

In this chapter we consider the following questions relating to the out-sourcing of library and information services:

- What are outsourcing and externalization?
- What are the uses of SLAs in outsourcing?
- Why do library and information services outsource?
- What do library and information services outsource?
- What issues arise once outsourcing is carried out?
- What are the effects on customers, staff and suppliers?
- What is the effect on the service?

What are outsourcing and externalization?

These are the definitions of outsourcing and externalization that we use in this chapter:

- *Outsourcing* is allowing another person or organization to provide a service or part of a service previously carried out inside the organization, usually on a contractual basis.
- *Externalization* is the delivery of a complete service, including the staffing and possibly the relocation of the service away from the purchaser's premises, by an external supplier.

You will find other definitions in use but they generally amount to the same thing. They all make the distinction between the *partial* and the *total* delivery of the library and information service by a third party or parties.

Outsourcing, externalization and service level agreements

The techniques that we have described earlier in this book will be important in ensuring that outsourcing (or externalization) achieves its purpose under good standards of management. An outsourcing agreement will be essentially the same as an SLA and can be used to govern the various aspects of the outsourced or externalized service.

However, the service specification must be carefully drawn up. Especially where the LIS is not consulted, there can be excessive concentration on the quantitative aspects of service (how many books are to be catalogued? how many enquiries are to be handled?) rather than the quality of service (are catalogued books delivered on time? can they be easily found from the catalogue descriptions? do users report satisfactory responses to enquiries?).

The specification must include a mechanism that provides the managers of the outsourced service with access to the policy-making process and the policy makers, so they can stay in touch with the business to receive information on new policies and in order to supply progress reports. A service level agreement is helpful in specifying the arrangements for communications and for managing the flow of information to the service managers.

In this section we have not included recommended wording, but have highlighted the issues that you need to consider. Because the agreements you reach are likely to be contractual in nature, we think it is important that your legal advisers draw up the wording, or approve the agreements that you draft.

The use of outsourcing and externalization

In the UK, many examples of outsourcing and externalization activities trace their roots to the political efforts in the 1980s and 1990s to reduce public sector costs, by means such as the reduction of staff levels and long-term costs.

However there are earlier antecedents in the USA. Herbert S. White recalls that the NASA Scientific and Technical Information Facility was completely contracted to an external supplier in the mid-1960s,[1] while one commentator[2] has traced the contracting out of library services in the USA to a 1955 federal government circular.[3]

The literature shows library and information services using outsourcing to help them to grapple with concepts such as 'value for money' and 'best value', and suggests that a justification for outsourcing that many use is that it allows them to focus on their core activities rather than on the delivery of minor services or areas of work that have low value and low interest.

But it can be argued that library and information services have long outsourced many of their activities, and probably for similar reasons. This includes a number of paraprofessional activities such as photocopying, book purchasing, handling journal subscriptions, and interlibrary loans. At a more basic level, work such as book jacketing and labelling has been bought in from book suppliers for many decades. Even some professional services such as cataloguing have been bought in for many years, through card supply services (such as the BNB card service) or from electronic suppliers such as OCLC.

Further developments have emerged, which library and information services have also had to manage at the same time as coping with the growth of outsourcing:

- cutbacks in funding which have led them to concentrate on core services
- local government reorganization
- growth of LIS purchasing consortia in a number of sectors, e.g. academia
- new business initiatives created by various partnerships, mergers, acquisitions, alliances and sponsorships in the book trade and in library and information services.

There are many examples where outsourcing in the LIS has been achieved with good results:

- security services
- cleaning services
- catering
- book binding
- looseleaf updating
- information technology/computer support
- subscription services.

There have been examples in public and private sector libraries where previous in-house providers have competed with private suppliers to offer such services. A frequent, though not universal, experience has been that in-house services have gained greater control of service costs, and there has been a benefit to both the LIS and the organization from the outsourcing process.

Issues in outsourcing

The LIS that uses outsourcing can find itself in a difficult position if it becomes a (possibly powerless) intermediary between the library user and the library supplier. It will have to put itself first in the position of supplier in order to discover what its users want, and then become the purchaser in order to pass these requirements to the external supplier.

In addition to dealing with this split role, the LIS also needs to consider some areas of vulnerability that need to be addressed in the agreement process.

Minimizing the risk

Identifying areas to outsource requires careful consideration, perhaps at more length than a management anxious for savings is willing to countenance. You do however need to ensure:

- that there is a sufficiently large supplier base able to offer the service
- that a large enough number of them are prepared to make a bid at a reasonable price

- that you have the resources to manage the resulting agreement or contract.

Otherwise you expose your organization to risk. The point that we made at the end of Chapter 1 becomes particularly important in this situation: if you draw up a specification so inflexible that it leads you into a one-to-one agreement with an inexperienced or poor supplier, you have effectively cut off the possibility of any worthwhile service development. Similarly if you choose to enter an area where there is only one supplier, you are at risk if that company's fortunes fail, and may find yourselves subject to unexpected price rises or shortfalls in service quality. The way of increasing the odds in your favour is to ensure that the specifications you issue for the service are pitched flexibly where necessary. This allows the potential supplier to organize a bid in terms that can be matched against your requirements and to identify possible economies of scale.

Use this book to help you to identify these areas for flexibility. Use the growing numbers of SLAs that have been published on the world wide web. Use the period of clarification and negotiation while concluding the contract in order to discover the supplier's strengths and what is already being done for other clients. Try to remove the risk along with the inessential elements of the specification.

You may need to bring in specialist help to arrive at the service definition, for example if you want to outsource web page authoring. Defining the service with this specialist may also help to identify alternative ways of meeting the requirement, or point out that not all the service needs to be outsourced in order to realize your targets.

Questions of ownership

In some circumstances, the question of ownership of the service, its stock, and even its staff can arise. Your agreement needs to state these ownerships precisely. Because of the nature of this agreement, we reinforce our earlier advice that your legal advisers formulate the words to be used.

Common arrangements are:

- Ownership of the stock (infrastructure, etc.) is transferred to the outsourcing company. In this case you need to consider what will happen at the end of the contract period, in order to avoid making an unplanned gift to a contractor you have dismissed. There will need to be safeguards, if you judge necessary, to prevent the contractor from selling off the stock during the contract period.
- The stock (infrastructure, etc.) is leased to the contractor, possibly for a peppercorn rent. In this way the ownership of the stock is never removed from the LIS. In the public sector this may be the only way that you can outsource.
- The LIS retains ownership of the stock, with the contractor providing personnel or accommodation.

Beware of writing the terms of the agreement so precisely that you prevent the library service from changing its location, or prevent the contractor from disposing of out-of-date reference books.

What do libraries outsource?

A recent survey[4] categorizes outsourced areas of LIS work into:

- IT
- technical services
- collection development
- document delivery
- electronic resources
- preservation.

Information technology

Libraries often depend on externalized or outsourced IT services. These may be in another part of the organization, or be part of a larger agreement with a third-party supplier. Library requirements are often overlooked, where for example the automated library system is run unsympathetically by a supplier that is far more interested in the widespread desktop applications (such as word-processing and spreadsheets) used throughout the organization. Outsourcing library IT may simply be outsourcing an unresolved problem, and despite the trend to converged library and IT services in academic libraries, the best protection for the LIS against these problems can lie in ensuring that the service specification for the overall contract contains explicit and well-expressed requirements. Specify the IT requirements for library and information services, records and archives management services, and knowledge or information management as needed, without being browbeaten to define your solutions in terms of standard software packages.

Internet service providers

A particular aspect of IT outsourcing is the agreement that you are likely to reach with your internet service provider (ISP). You will find that this does not constitute a formal contract, but an SLA, which has less force in law should you decide that service has been so abysmal that you wish to go to court. Service is widely reported to be poor, and ISPs are not keen to place themselves in a position of potential liability. Chapter 1 noted the survey that showed that 'SLAs that are met are the exception not the rule. Mostly businesses are not getting the service for which they are paying.'[5]

The levels of service quoted often look comfortably high, but because internet service is a 24-hour, 7-day operation, even a small shortfall from 100% connection can translate into uncomfortably long periods of downtime. An availability rate of 99.8% allows 17 hours' loss of service in a year; if all 17 hours come together the results could be catastrophic, so it may be wise to insist on an additional clause that will limit the length of time that will be tolerated in a single loss of service incident. You are likely to regard a time much longer than four hours as too long.

Look at the sample agreements that many ISPs post on the world wide web. You can include useful ideas from these in your own agreement. You may need to insist that you will not sign the standard agreement if its conditions are significantly less good than your requirements dictate.

Technical services

Suppliers are likely to make the running in service specification in this area, since there are many standard services that are (sometimes literally) bought off the shelf. Physical processing and cataloguing are long-established services but non-standard requirements are likely to be charged extra. The market is competitive, but margins are low and suppliers keep their costs down by expecting LIS customers to accept standard products. Nevertheless we believe it is worthwhile carrying out the specification process in order to identify the true requirements, and to decide whether the standard offer would in fact be acceptable.

Collection development

We described the Liverpool experiment in supplier-led book selection in Chapter 1. Here too, a specification is highly desirable, perhaps in the form of a published collection development policy indicating core areas and purchasing priorities in terms of types of publication.

Purchasing consortia are related to this area of work, and to technical services. The techniques of service level management can be useful in drawing up the agreements under which the consortia are set up, and of setting the timescales and other expectations of consortium members.

Document delivery

There is unlikely to be much scope for individual specification in this area, since national document supply services (such as the British Library Document Supply Centre in the UK, or INIST in France) have standard conditions for use, while commercial suppliers such as Uncover also have stated terms of trade. What may, however, be useful is a statement of the conditions for use of such services (i.e. guidelines for the choice between purchase and borrowing), which could form part of an overall service specification.

Electronic resources

Although some major collections have created published databases from their stock (such as DEVSIS, based on the British Library for Development Studies at the IDS, Brighton), in most cases there is no real prospect of in-house electronic resource creation beyond the normal catalogue. In effect, every consultation of an external database is a small act of outsourcing, and once again it is on the supplier's terms. We look further at this area in Chapter 10.

Preservation

Conservation and preservation are also specialist services where the supplier is likely to have standard terms, and possibly will have a better grasp of the technical detail required in the specification. However there is some scope for setting levels of service in other areas such as restoration or drying services. In case of emergency, the proper treatment of saturated materials may be more important than absolute speed, and the specification (again, drawn up with expert advice) should reflect the LIS's requirements.

Negotiating and agreeing the terms

The customers' expectations

An important element in approaching outsourcing is for the customer to understand the effect of outsourcing on service levels. Suppliers may be reluctant to go above particular levels, leading to the users' expectations being disappointed. An agreement should not be concluded with the external supplier until users are fully aware of the service levels being offered, and sign up to them.

A problem encountered at this stage is the need to explain the operation of various areas of library and information work to the library's users. While this is always important in negotiating an SLA for the operation of a library service, it becomes more so when services are outsourced. Library users may be expecting some dramatic improvement in service as a result of out-sourcing, whereas of course the time taken to deliver a journal issue from the publisher to the library (or the end-user) will be exactly the same whether the order has been placed by the library or by the outsourced supplier. The only area in this example where any difference can be made is in the time it takes to record the journal's arrival and apply circulation labels.

The LIS user community must understand that although they are, quite rightly, being invited to specify the levels, suppliers may choose to bid a lower level of service, or to negotiate additional costs for the gap between their serv-ice bid and the level required. The library manager's task is to ensure that the user community understands these constraints, and that the outsourc-ing agreement regulates only those areas that can be reasonably influenced by the supplier. Otherwise there will be an endless stream of pointless enquiries and allegations of poor service, and goodwill among all the parties will be endangered.

The most effective method of negotiation is likely to be for negotiations to be handled by the library service on behalf of the organization. If the organ-ization wishes to deal directly with the supplier, try to ensure that you are at least consulted on the wording of the documents before they are put to poten-tial suppliers. The assumption that only librarians are capable of understanding the ways of the publications trade is less common than it was, but it is still probably true that many professional purchasers do not intend to become experts on book purchasing and need to be supported by you. Your own inter-ests are best served by a specification that has been 'reality checked' by an LIS professional before issue and that does not create a stream of calls to the library manager seeking clarification of something the writer thought was clear. (Ear-lier, we recommended the use of a standard glossary.) Remember that in cases of doubt, many library suppliers still reach for the phone to call a librarian, who will understand what they are saying about the book trade, rather than a professional purchaser in the buying section.

Staff expectations

We discuss the effect of SLAs on staffing issues in Chapter 11. The threats that are felt when service level agreements are introduced seem even greater when there is the possibility of outsourcing or externalization, and the consequent possibility of job losses or radical changes of work patterns or routines. As a result the process of service specification is highly important in this situation. A precise specification allows members of staff to have a better idea of what should happen under the new arrangements, and provides evidence of what was agreed in negotiation.

Suppliers' expectations

Similarly the SLA provides the supplier with a record of the requirements that were agreed and the way in which any outsourced staff should be redeployed by the supplier. In the supplier's case too, the record of the negotiated agreement is an important document. The document should indicate to the supplier whether there is a problem as a result of a gap between the customer's expressed requirement and the supplier's own staff and technical resources.

A clear statement in an SLA of a requirement for the library to maintain membership of co-operative schemes or other interlibrary organizations may act as a warning to the supplier that negotiation with third parties is required. Statements concerning legal obligations such as the handling of personal data under the Data Protection Act will also highlight areas needing particular attention, and remind suppliers that they need to satisfy you that their procedures will shield you from legal challenge. If the supplier is known to handle information outside the European Union (for example in order to re-key catalogue card data, which contains personal information) then the agreement should set out the requirements to apply the necessary safeguards to comply with data protection law.

Providing feedback

Feedback has been identified as a problematic area in outsourcing of services. Particularly, if your user committee has been used to detailed monitoring reports, they may demand that the outsourced supplier is monitored to a similar level of scrutiny.

Bear in mind that the more complex the specification and the more performance indicators that are included, the more monitoring activity will fall upon the LIS staff. Monitoring criteria need to be useful as well as meaningful, and capable of being simply measured or judged. There are a number of documented instances where the costs of monitoring have outweighed any savings from outsourcing. Indeed there is evidence that where outsourcing is undertaken in an attempt to solve problems in the management chain, or problems of recruitment and retention, these problems are displaced rather than solved. As a result they become the subject of review meetings with the supplier when performance does not improve.

The supplier may be able to provide a number of standard reports, depending on the service. If there is a quality control system, you should be able to have copies of the output reports that apply to services provided to you. But if you are being asked to press the supplier to provide bespoke reports, you will need to intervene to protect his interests.

The reason that the supplier is chosen will normally have to do with his ability to supply you at lower cost and higher efficiency. Asking the supplier to provide non-standard reports from a bespoke monitoring system will interfere with procedures, and raise costs for you and perhaps for other customers. Persuade your LIS committee to accept standard outputs from the supplier, or ask for a quotation for the supplier to commission further standard reports. Resist efforts to get information that will suit nobody but the library committee, and that is almost certain to spoil the results for everyone.

Throughout this book we stress the importance of regular meetings. If you outsource, these are essential in order to build trust between your LIS and the supplier. You will also need meetings with the representatives of your users; but you will have to judge the right moment when (if ever) you decide to let your users near the supplier.

The effect on the service

The overall effect should, of course, be that the library and information service continues to provide the best possible range and quality of service to its users. They, in turn, should be pleased with the levels and quality of the library's service provision.

In fact the nature of the service will change if any degree of outsourcing takes place. With full externalization, the service may come from a different location – in which case the SLA clauses concerning timeliness and the position of service points take on new importance – or with a different staff, who will need to get to know the organization and its members (the library users). With outsourcing, library staff will have to get to know the supplier, and learn how his services fit into their own range of products for their library users. In either case there is likely to be a change of pace, and it may be as well to build in a period of grace before full levels have to be achieved. For example, the first quarter after the start of a new contract might not be counted towards service credits or penalties. However users need to be aware of this, and of any amendments to the complaints and escalation procedures during this time. Suppliers are likely to request some such concession even if the purchasing organization does not propose it.

Summary

This chapter has taken an overview of some of the issues raised by the outsourcing and externalization of library, information and related services. Both forms of outsourcing raise issues that can be addressed successfully using service level agreement techniques.

We have seen that outsourcing on a small scale has been happening for decades, and that even total externalization is not a new idea. But it is important to have good specifications of services, and to ensure that where internally supplied services remain, the staff there are consulted in reaching the service specification statement. It needs to be recognized that all parties – staff, users and suppliers – have issues, and that the service will inevitably change its nature.

Outsourcing can produce worthwhile savings, and improve the quality of the remaining staff, but it also has the potential to go badly wrong when requirements are not clearly spelt out, and negotiated and agreed by all parties.

9

Managing your suppliers

In this chapter you will find out:

- why your suppliers need to be managed
- who exactly your suppliers are
- how to define your requirements
- why you need to work closely with your supplier
- about complaints procedures.
- about corrupt gifts and payments
- about payments and audit
- about essential elements to be included in a contract
- about internal suppliers.

Why your suppliers need to be managed

When dealing with external suppliers you become the customer, so that your role is reversed from the role of supplier as described in previous chapters. However the same principles apply. You, as one of the parties to the SLA agreement, will have expectations and assumptions about the services you are expecting from your suppliers.

You need to be assured that all your suppliers can deliver the services you want at the time you need them. The LIS staff should not have to spend valuable time chasing their suppliers' staff. Any failure of delivery of services on the part of your suppliers could have a disastrous effect on your SLA with your organization.

Who exactly are your suppliers?

Many external organizations and a number of sections within your own organization will figure in your list of suppliers. By identifying likely suppliers, it may be possible to rationalize, or perhaps gain some financial advantages from your suppliers. They might include:

External suppliers

- booksellers
- subscription agents
- newsagents
- online suppliers
- CD-ROM suppliers
- inter-LIS loans delivery services
- translation services
- standard specifications body
- press cuttings services
- external enquiry services
- internet service providers.

Internal suppliers

- messengers/courier services
- reprographics service
- training department
- personnel department
- IT services
- press office
- publications sales office
- finance department.

Each supplier will need managing in a different way, but all will need an agreement spelling out the services required, the timescales and the performance levels (giving the percentage slippage allowed).

Defining your requirements

Think of all the steps in the process of a service being delivered to you when you are setting up the contract with a supplier who supports your internal SLA. State exactly what you want delivered and when it is required. For example, it is no good the newsagent delivering the morning papers at midday, when your customers want them on their desks by 9.00 a.m. An essential element of the supplier contract is detail, such as how often you want the products or services delivered. The alternative is constant chasing of the supplier to deliver to time. However, the agreement with the customer must reflect the practical possibility of service from the supplier, so that, in your negotiations with your customer, you may be able to extend the time by which a service is delivered. Reasonable delivery times for daily items will save courier charges, while having journals to which you are subscribing delivered by the supplier once a week instead of daily may save further on costs (which may well be loaded for daily deliveries), or allow the use of consolidation services for further savings.

Once you have decided and agreed on the timing of deliveries and what is being delivered, then the next thing you need to think about is the quality of the service: the standards and the percentage of acceptable slippage.

Premium service

If you require more urgent delivery of services than the supplier's normal service, then you need to set out in your contract/SLA the parameters of what you require and the pricing structure. For example, you may wish to have the facility to use an immediate or urgent delivery document supply service using fax or e-mail. A number of these services are available (such as from the British Library Document Supply Centre (BLDSC) or UnCover), but at a premium price. You will need to establish an agreement with the supplier, either using the standard contract or an agreed variation, perhaps specifying a contact person, and the price per document or page delivered. Again, you will need to define the agreed standards and acceptable percentage slippages against time or request fulfilment rate.

Change control procedure

Should you want to change any of the currently agreed service deliveries, then you must ensure that any changes are agreed between all parties. The contract/SLA must be amended, and all staff on both sides notified of the changes. Downstream, if this change affects your own users, then they must be informed: and, if these changes agreed with the suppliers affect the contract/SLA you have with users, then this in turn will need altering. It is essential that the agreement with your users and the contracts with your suppliers remain in step.

It would be a sensible step to create an archive of contracts and agreements, with a record of changes (version control) so that it is clear what was agreed on any given date, and giving rapid reference to changes to the agreement. Include a section at the end of the document for listing changes with their dates, and, if keeping a word processed copy, ensure that the date is printed on every page, together with the version number. Be sure that if the program shows the date of printing on the page, the document also contains the date on which the document was agreed, and that this is kept as a fixed data item.

The agreement

Terms, conditions and definitions

You will need to have a clear understanding of the terms and conditions of the supplier agreement, which must state that any such terms can be varied only with the written agreement of your organization. In case of dispute, it is the written and signed version that will be referred to, not any ad hoc interpretation, or favours agreed by members of the supplier's staff without reference to their management.

Define your terms

We drew attention earlier to the need for careful definition, if necessary by reference to a standard glossary such as the BS 7408. The same principle applies here, and the vocabulary should be extended to include terminology used in reaching a contractual agreement with a supplier. For example:

- 'contractor' means the person/company to whom the contract/SLA is issued
- 'services' means the service to be provided and shall, where the context admits it, include any materials, articles or goods to be supplied
- 'premises' means the location where the services are to be performed
- 'contract' means the contract between the organization and the supplier/contractor.

As the following case study shows, this can be of vital importance in managing the contract.

Case study

When organization M contracted with supplier N for publications supply, the LIS users soon began to complain that the delivery speed for urgent requests had dropped noticeably. The LIS complained to supplier N that performance was below the agreed standard, but the supplier replied that this was normal quality for urgent requests. It transpired that the supplier used the term 'rush' to denote orders required within 24–48 hours and imposed an additional delivery and service charge for these. The LIS was then faced with the need to pay (and recover from customers) an unexpected additional sum to cover the service charges on material that its previous supplier had handled at no extra cost. The assumption that the term 'urgent' carried the same meaning to both parties turned out to be quite wrong.

Complaints procedure

Your contract or agreement with the supplier should also contain a complaints procedure, should the service fail in any way. You will need, as in the agreement with your own customers, an escalation procedure.

Inspection of premises and nature of services

Before the agreement is set up, you will need to allow the suppliers/contractors to visit the premises and understand the nature and extent of the services you require. Your organization should grant reasonable access for this purpose.

You should also make sure that the suppliers/contractors clearly understand that, as contractors, they are acting solely as suppliers and not as the agents of your organization.

> **Nothing in a contract/SLA shall impose any liability on XYZ organization, or any liability incurred by the supplier/contractor to any other person, but this shall not be taken to exclude or limit any liability of the organization to the supplier/contractor that may arise by virtue of either a breach of the contract/SLA or any negligence on the part of the organization, its staff or its agents.**

You may wish to add a further rider which insists that the contractor imposes a similar requirement on any subcontractor employed. It is important that nobody purports to speak for you without your agreement and authorization. There is more on the question of subcontractors below.

Contractor's personnel

Should you require the supplier/contractor to give the names of any persons involved in the contract/SLA, specifying the capacities in which they are concerned with it, you should ensure that your contract/SLA contains a statement to that effect. You will need to make a decision whether the supplier/contractor has to bear the costs for these actions. Where the reason for doing this could be argued to be a result of your stringent security requirements, it may be unreasonable to pass the cost to the contractor. You may also wish to include the right to exclude any or all of the contractor's personnel on security grounds.

Manner of carrying out the services

You would be wise to ensure that the agreement specifies that the supplier/contractor may not make a delivery of materials, plant or other items, or commence work on your organization's premises without obtaining your organization's prior consent. This may apply before, during or after the contract; the wording should indicate which. (As examples, you might not wish for a new contractor to deliver new computer equipment in advance of a contract when you have no secure storage, or for a supplier to use spare capacity to deliver new publications in the evening when out-of-hours security is in force.) You may further wish to include wording ensuring that nothing is removed after the end of the contract without your agreement.

Time of commencement of services

You will need to agree on the exact dates and times contracted and for the period of the contract or agreement, but you may from time to time ask the supplier/contractor to execute the services in a different manner or at different times (such as weekends). This should be put in writing whenever this occurs.

Payment

Agreement must be reached about exactly when payments are to be made. Normal practice is to allow 30 days from the receipt of invoices, which are submitted monthly in arrears for work completed to your organization's satisfaction. You will also need to let your supplier/contractor know to whom complaints about late payment should be made. You should also inform the supplier/contractor that, if they are not satisfied, they should complain to the head of financial services (or someone of similar standing).

Value-added tax

Where applicable, VAT should be shown separately on all invoices sent to you, but note that each finance department may work differently. You may have to explain carefully to your finance section that some suppliers have agreements with HM Customs and Excise that allow them to apply VAT to only part of subscriptions or charges, so that VAT equivalent to one-half or one-quarter of the standard rate may apply to your invoices.

Audit

For audit purposes, your supplier/contractor should keep and maintain for two years (or as specified by your finance department) complete records of all expenditures that are reimbursable by the organization for the hours worked and the costs involved in executing the services. If you are working in a governmental environment, then National Audit Office staff or members of your own organization may need to interview personnel to obtain appropriate oral explanations of documents. Here you will need to let the supplier/contractor know that they must allow access to such personnel.

Corrupt gifts and payments

If your organization has rules and regulations on the acceptance of gifts or payments from external parties, then the supplier/contractor must be informed. There is a fairly standard form of wording that is widely used, to the effect that the supplier/contractor must not offer any gift or consideration of any kind, as an inducement or reward for doing or refraining from doing, any act in relation to the obtaining or execution of this or any other order or contract/SLA from your organization. You should also make the supplier/contractor aware that any breach of the above will entitle the organization to terminate the contract/SLA and recover from the supplier/contractor the amount of any loss resulting from such termination. It should also be pointed out, if appropriate, that the criminal offence provisions of the Prevention of Corruption Act may apply.

The organization probably has a freer policy on the acceptance of minor gifts at Christmas and broad guidelines could usefully be included in the contract. The boundary may be hazily drawn: a small pocket diary may be acceptable while a leather desk diary would not. In cases of doubt, it is worthwhile seeking central guidance, since the acceptable norms for gifts or entertainment in some sectors (for example journalism or advertising) may appear to vary considerably from those in others.

Patents and information

Other areas to watch are those concerning intellectual property. The supplier/contractor must not infringe any patent, trademark, registered design, copyright or other right in the nature of industrial property and you need to put this in the contract/SLA.

You should take careful note of the provisions of the Copyright Designs and Patents Act 1988, which made substantial changes to the ownership rights of the intellectual property in work done under contract; seek legal advice if necessary. Ensure that copyright is not infringed by any supplier working under contract to you, and seek clarification if you are unsure whether the protection of any copyright licence you hold extends to contractors on your premises. Check each licence; what suits one licensing agency may not be acceptable to the others.

Intellectual property rights have become a major issue for organizations whose staff create web pages. There is a continuing debate over the widespread practice of copying code from other sites in order to reproduce an effect or design that the author admires there. You may decide to insert a clause to the effect either that all code should be original in nature (given the nature of HTML and other codes, there is likely to be a lot of similarity between the actual code on two different pages), or that any extensive use of code from other sites should be with the permission of the site owner if the code is not specifically advertised as public domain.

Indemnity and insurance

You will need to insert a clause about indemnity, including information about your employer's liability insurance. Look into your own organization's approach both to the contractor's personnel working on your premises and to any incident taking place on your premises involving a contractor or a member of the public. Ensure that the health and safety legislation is clearly understood by all workers, both internal and contract staff.

Discrimination

In the UK, the contract or agreement with your contractor will also require clauses regarding discrimination in employment. You need to take account of the Race Relations Act 1976 (together, if relevant, with the Race Relations (Amendment) Act 2000), the Disability Discrimination Act 1995, and the Welsh Language Act 1993.

Charities

You should ensure that any contractor that appears to act directly for you complies with the requirements of the Charities Act 1993 by ensuring that full details of your charitable status appear on any official documents (including cheques and orders 'purporting to be signed on behalf of the charity').

Official Secrets Acts and confidentiality

Contractors and suppliers to the public sector in the UK need to be made aware of the provisions of the Official Secrets Act and may be required to sign the Act. In many sectors, confidentiality requirements are in place and the contractor must be required to meet the same standard as your own staff.

Computer misuse, data protection and freedom of information

You need to ensure that contractors and suppliers accept their responsibilities under the Computer Misuse Act 1990 and the Data Protection Act 1998. There may be further obligations under the Freedom of Information Act 2000 if publicly funded bodies are involved: note that this Act extends to organizations such as universities and colleges as well as to the more obvious government departments and local authorities. Some organizations, for example the National Health Service, have a range of further regulations that encompass the requirements of these Acts of Parliament, and other laws that regulate their particular activity.

Termination of the contract or agreement: costs and their recovery

You will need to have extensive provision regarding the termination of the contract or agreement. This will include details of timing, such as periods of notice, or directions on allocation of the costs involved. There may also be details of how the sums of money involved are to be recovered.

Assignment and subcontracting

You should specify that the contractor/supplier must have your organization's prior written consent before assigning or subcontracting work. You must insist that any subcontracting will not relieve your contractor/supplier of the relevant responsibilities, and that prompt payment should be made to any subcontractor.

Transmission of notices

You must finalize agreement on how notices from and to the contractor or supplier will be handled: by fax, by hand, or by registered or recorded delivery mail, for example. This is very important, especially when many staff members of both parties may be involved. This will ensure that any verbal discussions are clarified, transmitted and received accurately. We assume, of course, that your organization has in place good records management procedures, including service level management, to maintain suitable records of these communications.

Arbitration

The contract or agreement should specify how the arbitration process, if invoked, will be handled, and by whom. Similar considerations apply as for internal disputes, but remember that contracts in this section may be enforceable in law.

Legitimacy of the workforce

You will need to ensure that persons employed by the contractor/supplier and any subcontractor are entitled to obtain employment in the UK, and are not claiming or receiving unemployment benefit or any other relevant benefits. You also need to ensure that these people are entitled to live and work in the United Kingdom, under the terms of the Asylum and Immigration Act 1996. This act created a new criminal offence for employers in cases where employees started work for an employer on or after 27 January 1997 and did not have this entitlement.

Governing law

You should state that conditions in the contract are governed by and constructed in accordance with UK law, or whichever other legal system is adopted in your organization. Take into consideration the question of where legal action might be taken should you need to enforce the contract in a court of law.

Essential contract elements

A checklist of essential elements for a contract with an external supplier would include:

- the precise nature of each function or service being provided
- the volumes and quality to be achieved for each of the services
- whether optional services are on offer to you, and if so, what they are and what they cost
- what procedures should be followed if it becomes necessary to vary the terms of the contract/SLA
- where applicable, the response times to be achieved by the supplier when receiving your requests for assistance
- the system of charging: the basis of charges, what has to be paid and how
- the procedure for settling disputes
- the period of notice of termination
- insurance liability (if relevant)
- what resources, information or other help you may have to provide
- contact points for both parties.

In addition to this checklist, there is likely to be a list of required or preferred terms within your sector (such as that from the Central Unit on Purchasing Guidance for the UK central government sector) and terms from this will have to be incorporated, probably following a required wording.

The organization may well require financial information about the supplier and may require certain guarantees or other wording to be included.

Internal suppliers

Many of these aspects apply to internal suppliers, although corporate legal and personnel services will take care of many of the questions for you. You may find some changes to the procedures described here if an internal supplier is used: for example, some organizations in the public sector incorporate an element into the cost calculations that equates to the sum that an external supplier would have charged for VAT. Use the descriptions above to see which items are relevant to your position in relation to other sections of your organization.

Apply your knowledge of SLAs to any documents you are given, and do not sign a substandard agreement, especially if you find you will be suffering loss of service quality or an increase in unnecessary bureaucracy as a result!

Summary

There are a large number of legal and quasilegal aspects to dealing with suppliers that you need to cover in a service level agreement. You do not need to be a legal expert to deal with this aspect of the work, but you do need access to one. We have indicated a range of issues where you need to be satisfied, either that you have covered the risk, or that you do not need to concern yourself with the question. Use this as a checklist, and ask your advisers whether there are any other points that you need to cover in dealing with an external supplier.

Do not worry. Problems do not occur every day, and solving them is a learning experience both for you and for the supplier.

10
MANAGING YOUR E-SUPPLIERS

In this chapter we describe:

- the development of electronic services
- some specific details of electronic service supply that should be in your SLA
- the differences between 'normal' supplying and e-supplying
- how to define your requirements
- the things to watch.

The development of electronic services

The range of electronic services available to LIS has developed rapidly and includes 'traditional' online databases, tape services and other means of distributing data, CD-ROMs and internet-based services. There is a range of access options, so that subscription agents and others have been able to extend their services to customers, and frequently offer web-based services rather than simply providing administrative services based around the delivery of printed publications.

For example:

- SilverPlatter offer access to over 300 of their own and partner publishers' databases, such as the world-renowned OSH-ROM product, which contains six international bibliographic databases containing over 1.9 million records, through their ERL (Electronic Reference Library) Partner Hosted Server.

- Dialog@SiteServer provides access to over 80 Dialog databases, covering subjects including environment, chemistry, health and safety.

Library and information services can outsource to subscription agents the day-to-day provision of databases, but the complexity of the services should already be apparent. The service level agreement offers an excellent means of specifying what is required, and managing its delivery.

Some specific details of electronic service supply that should be included in your SLA

Electronic services have become an integral part of the range of services that a library and information service offers. The range of services that is widely available includes:

- e-journals
- e-document delivery
- e-enquiry services
- e-databases (previously CD-ROM).

As in all dealings with suppliers you must negotiate and evaluate all the services needed before you finally purchase. You will need to negotiate to ensure the best price and service delivery and you will need to constantly monitor e-delivery. Your SLA will record the outcome of the negotiations and will set the parameters for monitoring.

Unlike books and journals, e-services do not arrive as physical documents in the library so you will need to ensure that your SLA records:

- the alerting or notification system that will be used to inform you of the publication date of the latest edition of a journal
- the actions to be taken if the computer systems fail.

Each supplier will need managing in a different way, but all will need an agreement that spells out:

- the services required
- the timescales
- the performance levels (identifying a means of measuring service, agreeing the amount of slippage allowed, and recording performance).

Each of the types of e-supply has particular issues associated with it.

e-journals

There has been a huge growth in the number of electronic journals since 1995. Registration and access procedures were very cumbersome at first. Services are now constantly improving through the use of new technology, with improvements in searching and growing integration with other electronic services.

Case study

SwetsNet*Navigator* offers aggregated access to electronic journals through a single interface, and provides cross searching of content with additional functionality. It offers over 3100 full-text titles from over 60 publishers, and full-text back files for up to five years allow the user to search for retrospective information. Besides the full-text service there is also a large database where it is possible to browse the contents of about 15,000 titles.

The search facility offers both basic and advanced interfaces and also allows users to specify an SDI (Selective Dissemination of Information) alerting service. A further option allows users to select titles of interest at the Table of Contents (ToC) level, allowing them to define their own database of titles covered.

Contents page alerting allows organizations to receive alerts of items of specific interest. The service offers usage statistics to allow managers to ensure that the resources invested in the service are being well used. Subsets can be created and titles allocated to particular users, such as a section or laboratory that wishes to receive an agreed set of titles.

Pages of hyperlinks allow users to view individual articles by following a series of connected indexes, by title, year and issue, giving access to a choice of abstract or full text. Full search facilities are provided, as well as links to over 300 other bibliographic databases from a range of organizations. Users can create links from their own catalogues to full text within the service or held on another supplier's databases. Finally there are delivery options to choose from.

This overview of a typical service demonstrates the level of complexity that is frequently found when specifying electronic services. This complexity is deepened by the fact that different user groups may require varying levels of service, with related issues of cost and monitoring.

All the options chosen need to be specified in the SLA, particularly if there are licence conditions relating to particular groups of users that restrict access to or use of the data. Typical issues might be the definition of the users within the organization, for example do distance learners on other campuses qualify for the site licence, and do members of faculty working at home, or home workers within a research company, also qualify?

It is particularly important that 'dead end' links are eliminated. Subscription agents are keen to ensure that their databases are free of this problem, knowing the adverse effect that faulty links can bring. A challenge is to create a global standard to link local, national and international data in primary and secondary literature, and grey literature. The International Standard Serial Number (ISSN) has strong potential to provide a standard for some publications, but it does not apply universally; however you could usefully include it (or other systems such as CODEN) in specifying the data sets that you define for managing your e-collection.

When setting up an e-journal delivery agreement you may be given the following options for a subscription:

* e-journal and print version
* e-journal title and abstracts
* e-journal full text access
* e-journal archive access.

If for instance you have already in your information service the back files of a particular journal, consider if you really need them. If you have a space problem, you may wish to access the e-journal back files instead of keeping, maintaining and paying for storage space. Once you have made the decisions you will need to write the requirements into the SLA. Other requirements to be specified are likely to include:

* the number of simultaneous users (both in your own and any consortia member organization)
* the length of the subscription period (as with journal subscriptions you may get discounts for signing up for two or more years)
* who will be responsible for the password control
* who will be the contact for the consortia
* who will be responsible for receipt of messages from the supplier
* who be responsible for information and instructions to the supplier.

e-databases

As with e-journals, the SLA will need to state:

* the number of simultaneous users (both in your own and any consortia member organization)
* the length of the subscription period (and any discounts for signing up for two or more years)
* who will be responsible for the password control
* who will be the contact for the consortia

- who will be responsible for receipt of messages from the supplier
- who be responsible for information and instructions to the supplier.

If you or members of a consortium have had a previous subscription to a database title on CD-ROM that had an archive disc, you will need to negotiate and record how this archive data is to be searched in future.

Especially in a large user group, you need to assess the likely number of simultaneous users carefully. There may be only a small number of specialist users who will use particular types of database that are available on a large network. For example, a legal database may be of use only to your lawyers and the library, even though there may be 5000 workstations on the network, and you may need to negotiate carefully if the supplier suggests you should license every user of the network rather than perhaps 20 simultaneous users. However some services take a more realistic view of the potential use of their data and have only two or three bands of simultaneous user licence, one of which is standalone single machine.

Suppliers also have varying definitions of the boundaries of the user community. These, for example, are some of the permutations that e-suppliers apply in their licensing and access policies:

- The licence covers all users within the organization.
- The licence covers all users within the organization and working on its office premises (i.e. home workers and people working away from the office or campus are excluded even if they are connected to the office network via a laptop or mobile link).
- The licence covers all users within the organization but each campus or office counts as a separate location and is licensed separately.
- The licence covers only named users within the organization (who may be identified to the supplier's system by the IP address of their computer – and that may require you to use standalone access only in order to present a consistent IP address to the remote computer when logging on).

There are, obviously, further permutations along these lines: check what is offered, see whether any negotiation is possible, and prepare to explain to your users why some databases are universally available while others are restricted in one of several ways!

e-document delivery

A range of such services is available from organizations such as the British Library Document Supply Centre, OVID, Uncover, etc. Many of these have standard terms of use but some negotiation may be possible, especially if you are representing a consortium.

Technical infrastructure

When setting up an e-document delivery agreement you may be given a number of options. First, should the document be delivered direct to the customer, or to the information service for onward transmission?

Second, you have a range of format options in an integrated infrastructure for a library and information service based on e-delivery of documents. The data may be full text in a variety of file types – HTML (HyperText Markup Language, the most common web page writing format), pdf (Portable Document Format, Abode's proprietary format that shows an image of the page with photographic accuracy), XML (eXtensible Markup Language, a more recent format that is a kind of extended HTML) among many examples – or it may only exist as an abstract.

The service definition for your services needs to take account of the formats in which your required journal articles (and other documents) are available. (In contrast, do not waste time on the formats that cannot anyway be handled by your network.) The supply of audiovisual materials may cause particular issues for technical reasons (such as the competing formats for video and audio streaming) and in respect of licensing the use of broadcast and other copyright content.

Also be clear whose responsibility it is to provide and whose to license any special software required to view articles or documents. While the Adobe Acrobat reader is widely and freely available, you will have more problems with any proprietary reader software offered, especially if it needs to be placed on a network or on many computers in order to allow library users to read the documents sent to them. What are the costs, both of buying and/or licensing the software, and (the hidden costs of) installing and maintaining the software on your computers?

Case study

A medium-sized LIS circulated their journals but knew they could take up to two years to reach all customers after initial issue. The journals were untraceable, and except for the first few on the circulation list, many users never saw the journals. The LIS were also going to the British Library for titles that were already circulating to the users. A solution was to keep the journals in the LIS, circulate the tables of contents to the users, and then photocopy the article(s) required.

By taking out an e-subscription the LIS was able to offer a better service. Contents pages were issued electronically via the intranet, containing hot links to the abstracts and then the full text. These actions increased the awareness of the many services provided by the LIS and raised the profile of the service on the intranet.

Application service providers

You may need to include a section in your SLA about the use of ASPs. These are companies that hold a range of software applications on their server computers, and license the use of that software to users who can access using the internet as a linking channel. You might, for example, decide that you need to use computer-assisted drawing software to prepare plans of a branch library, but that you do not wish to pay the cost of purchasing and installing a suitable program. An ASP will provide you with a defined period of access to the package (perhaps a week or a month) at a stated cost. However the software is not physically installed on your computer, and you work through the internet to reach the supplier's computer where the software resides.

As with internet service providers, there are issues of service availability: if anything, the need for high availability is even more critical, since the period of use for most software is short. Downtime during peak business hours is a serious issue, as valuable working time will be lost from the time paid for.

Adopt the same strategies as for internet service providers, but insist particularly on availability guarantees, and additional compensating time in case of service failure. Ensure here that all agreements mesh, so that your use of ASPs' service is supported on any computers where rented software is being accessed.

Defining your requirements

The sections above have shown that all the steps in service delivery must be taken into account when you are setting up the contract or service level agreement with a e-supplier whose services you need to support your internal SLA. It is clear that far more detail may need to be included in the agreement for electronic services, and that you will need to consider the effect of introducing these services on existing agreements. In many cases the computer system that will accept electronic products is owned by another part of the organization and the LIS's requirements may not be foremost in the attentions of the system managers.

State exactly what you want delivered and when it is required. For example, it is no good for the latest edition of an e-journal to be delivered without any alert to signal its arrival, so the devil is truly in the detail. The alternative is for the LIS to be constantly chasing suppliers to deliver to time or to give notice of the arrival of updates and new products. Your internal agreement may be sufficiently flexible, or negotiable, to allow you to vary delivery times to suit changes in your supplier's schedule.

Once you are satisfied with these aspects you can move on to assure the quality of the service to your customers.

Things to watch: checking the details

Adopting e-services will take some of the repetitive work away from the LIS, but remember that attention must be given to all the details that are discussed in Chapter 9 'Managing your suppliers'. The issues we consider in this chapter need to be addressed in addition to these more general aspects of supplier management, so there is considerable work to do at the start of an e-supply contract or agreement. However, time and effort spent on getting the SLA right at the outset will save time and effort in the long run that will allow LIS staff to work productively on developing other value-added services.

The contract

As we have just noted, the contract for e-supplies will need to cover all the elements that we discussed in the more general chapter on supplier management. There we saw that the contract (or agreement, which is all an ASP is likely to offer) should aim to define:

- the precise nature of each function or service being provided
- the volumes and quality to be achieved for each of the services
- whether optional services are on offer to you, and if so, what they are and what they cost
- what procedures should be followed if it becomes necessary to vary the agreement
- where applicable, the response times to be achieved by the supplier when receiving your requests
- the system of charging: the basis of charges, what has to be paid and how this is to be paid
- the procedure for settling disputes
- the period of notice of termination
- what resources, information or other help you may have to provide
- contact points for both parties, including escalation procedures.

The contract for e-services will need to include a number of further details, as relevant:

- format of files (file types) being provided
- details of any special software required, including licensing and cost issues
- licensing conditions for the document content, and conditions of onward transmission of document files to other users.

Consortia services

Consortium buying can have considerable financial advantages, both in terms of cash savings and of increased flexibility in licensing. Suppliers are increasingly used to working in this way, recognizing that the increased levels of business compensate for the reduced margins. You may choose to form a consortium, to join an existing organization, or perhaps even to use the supplier's facilities to create a single point of contact for a group of library purchasers. You need to take a number of issues into consideration here, such as the similarity of accounting and information technology systems, and we suggest that you should negotiate and agree the terms of the consortium management before you tackle the suppliers. Use local informal networks to discover whether other potential partners could join you and increase your buying and bargaining power.

Many e-subscription agents are providing consortia services, whether for a multinational organization working through a number of sites collecting and collating data, or for a number of similar organizations that decide to purchase and have access together to the same data sources.

The agents' role is to:

- collect the consortium data (such as numbers of libraries, sites, title needs, numbers of copies taken)
- obtain pricing and licensing proposals from publishers
- handle the day-to-day subscription processing

- provide consortium members with the required access to electronic information resources.

An e-agent thus takes away the burden of administration from the library and information service. They manage licences from each publisher, organize access to journals, and calculate the price per publication across multiple sites, whether this is for cross-access from several sites or independent access to individual journals by specific sites or even single computers. They organize the technical infrastructure, make subscription payments and carry out claiming, invoicing, sourcing and subscription management. The customer can frequently receive service information and technical support online.

As the customer is a consortium, your role is reversed from that of supplier but the same principles apply. You, as one of the parties to the SLA agreement, will have expectations and assumptions about the services you are expecting from your suppliers. Your problem is to maintain the balance between your own users' requirements and those of other partners in the purchasing consortium. You may need to negotiate terms for some products with other consortium members, as well as with suppliers and your own customers.

You need to be assured that your own interests are adequately covered within the terms the consortium reaches with your suppliers. Will you receive the services you want at the time you need them? Your staff should not have to spend valuable time chasing the suppliers' staff, but nor, if they are obliged to deal with the supplier at second hand through the consortium management office, should they have problems getting a fast remedy if an individual supplier is failing. Any such delivery failure could have a disastrous effect on your own internal SLA.

Summary

This is a new and exciting area of library management. Electronic services are immediate, and can be called to any desktop when needed. They have the potential to break away from the 'one book, one reader' model to a new way of working where several people can, subject to the terms of licences, have simultaneous access to the same resource at the same time and work on it together. The many and varied e-services that we have described will give your LIS more opportunities to innovate and deliver new kinds of service for your customers.

Compiling an SLA will help you to clarify your way of working, not only within your own LIS but in dealing with your customers, your e-suppliers, and even with other members of a purchasing consortium.

Points on which to reflect

- Are your definitions understood both by your customer and your e-suppliers?
- Have you have covered as wide a range of issues as possible for inclusion in your SLA?
- Have you read all the contracts and licences for e-services that you intend to use, and ensured that there are no problems?

Remember to seek help on technical issues that you do not understand! Also add to and develop the sections above depending on your LIS's circumstances.

11
MANAGING STAFF

In this chapter you will find out:

- why staff criticize the new system
- ways of avoiding conflict
- opportunities for all.

The management of staff is a vital element in your plans to introduce service level agreements. If the staff are unwilling or unhappy, the introduction and operation of SLAs are likely to be beset by squabbles over petty interpretation of the letter of the agreement, and the service is likely to be affected by a sense of reduced co-operation and inflexibility. Customers will be sure to notice, and the positive benefits of the SLA will be overlooked as all parties struggle to overcome these negative aspects.

Consider your staff as being divided into two types: those who are active in spreading new ideas and ways of working, and those who are passive and get their ideas by 'buying' them from other members of staff. The active staff, the opinion setters and the strong characters, are those who can prove the most difficult if they take against working with service level agreements, so it pays to take care that they understand fully what the changes are all about.

Frequently these are the staff who form the links between the new contractor and the organization at large. If the contract is let in such a way that the LIS is the point of contact for publications orders and other purchases, a difficult attitude or any expression of hostility towards the new arrangements will be immediately obvious to your customers, and quite probably to other members of your organization.

One reason for hostility may be that the new arrangements involve managing the transition from one type of service to another – and that this is just sheer hard work for the people at the front line. You need to acknowledge that in the transition period, and when the library customers are getting used to the new ways of working, there can be considerable stress involved, which mere payment for the overtime hours will not necessarily address. Find some other way, either involving money or time off, or else telling the organization as a whole about the excellent service that they continue to receive thanks to the effort that these members of staff have put in. This may be a message that can be put out through one of the communications channels that we discuss in Chapter 12.

Problems that staff can cause

How can staff cause problems for the management of service level agreements? The following have been reported in practice.

Criticism of the new system

Members of staff opposed to change may take every opportunity to tell customers that the new ways are not sensible, or get in the way of providing the kind of service that the library has traditionally given the customer. If these are key staff, this can quickly undermine the perception of the quality of the library, and begin to cast doubt on the soundness of management if an apparently unfavourable contract has been entered. Staff who are known to be critical in this fashion need to be handled tactfully but firmly. They must realize that the alternative is not to scrap the SLA but to find ways to manage it flexibly. It would have been an idea, of course, to keep staff aware of the progress of negotiations, so that they were prepared for the changes.

Adoption of a 'jobsworth' attitude

Members of staff may draw attention to the shortcomings of the new system, particularly its apparent inflexibilities, again telling customers that it is now beyond the staff's ability to provide the kind of service that used to be available ('it's more than my job's worth to do that now'). But rather than overt hostility, this type of behaviour tends towards a kind of conspiracy, in which the library staff and customers are seen to collude against the inept library management that has agreed to such an inflexible arrangement. The awkward staff can further conspire with the customer to do a favour ('just this once, then') that makes the customer into a client of the member of staff rather than of the library as a whole. Again, it would be best to demonstrate the flexibility of the service from the outset, and ensure that customers as well as library staff know that the existence of the agreement does not condemn every transaction to being some long drawn-out process that delays simple orders for weeks.

Criticism of suppliers

Particularly difficult is the member of staff who openly criticizes the new suppliers. Sometimes this comes out in the form of explicit adverse criticism ('we never had these problems with the old supplier'); otherwise it is straightforward carping about anything that goes wrong, like incorrect billing. Suppliers are unlikely to be pleased if this gets back to them, and even less pleased if it gets to other organizations that are considering doing business with them. If there are problems, your staff must be objective, and ensure that those problems are sorted out. The supplier must have the chance to put things right – we are, after all, considering a contract that will have appropriate clauses to require and to allow this to happen. Staff need to be made aware that their first action when there are problems must be to get on to the supplier to correct matters, not to start criticizing.

'Us and them'

Most staff are quite happy to work together with a supplier and present a uni-
fied face to the library customer, so that when there are supply problems the
user is left with the feeling that library and serials agent or bookshop are working together to solve them. Service level agreements can have the effect of
creating a division in the customer's perception in what had previously been
a single spectrum working to provide his or her information needs. As we
began to see above, it is now 'them' who are causing a problem by their failure to work to the same methods as the previous supplier, or 'us' who are
having to put up with poor service that disappoints our customers.

As well as demonstrating flexibility, you may need to challenge members
of staff who spread this kind of view through individual discussions. They
need to see that there is no difference between the new relationship and that
with any other previous supplier. Suppliers are in business to succeed and –
let's face it – to make a profit, and any company that consistently ignores the
requirements of its customers will pretty soon fail. It may be hard going for
a few weeks, but both supplier and library have the same long-term aim. By
creating division, your staff members are not giving either you or your suppliers a fair run at the issues.

Issues that staff may raise

Staff may also raise issues about the service level agreement directly with their
managers. Among the issues that have arisen in libraries are these.

Resentment over the work involved

The introduction of service level management does lead to additional work,
it must be agreed. Or rather it leads to different tasks being done when others may no longer be needed. Your staff may not be servicing the books any
longer by adding plastic covers or labels, or you may decide to accept cataloguing-
in-publication information and let the supplier apply class labels accordingly.
Instead you may use some of the time saved to carry out a quality check on

151

the supplier, perhaps by sampling every tenth item and performing checks on various elements of the servicing. The rest of the time saved can be put into new activities that generate further custom for the LIS and make its position more secure. However it can happen that the new work of checking becomes more noticeable than the saving in work passed to the supplier, or the new work that others are doing. It must be made clear what changes have taken place across the spectrum, so that staff can be pleased about the work they are saved (and the quality of the supplier's work, it must be hoped) rather than annoyed that they appear to have even more work. If work is properly designed, library staff will still have ultimate control through the quality checking process of what is being delivered to the customer.

'Difficulties fall to the LIS staff'

Staff may perceive themselves as taking the blame for any shortcomings in the service, when previously a call to the supplier would probably have sorted matters out amicably and quickly. The SLA in effect acts as a barrier to the library customer, who does not have a direct role in the agreement and cannot take complaints to the supplier directly. The fact that there is now a formal document setting out rights and responsibilities can also lead to entrenched attitudes being taken, and the library staff find themselves in the position of needing to interpret the SLA for both the supplier ('what we meant by that clause was . . .') and the library user ('when they say this, what the suppliers mean is . . .'). There is a feeling of being pig-in-the-middle that can quickly escalate into one of the behaviours we examined above. Tactics for dealing with this should include a plan for communication with library customers, to explain how problems are to be resolved. Simple tactics like staff rostering can ensure that the same person does not always handle complaints.

'Eating into professional time'

We have encountered professional staff who consider that this kind of management interferes with the 'real' work of a qualified librarian, and should be left to support staff or accountants. There is not really a remedy for dealing with this attitude, other than to record that in the 21st century, this is part of what library management is about. Library managers need to demonstrate their ability to deliver best value for money, and to monitor the way that they do this: service level agreements provide a good tool for doing so, and there is no excuse for attitudes like this.

TUPE

The results of the TUPE process – the transfer of staff from library to supplier or another employer under the Transfer of Undertakings–Protection of Employment Regulations – can also produce staff problems. Handling the process can be difficult for library managers, particularly if part of the team is being moved compulsorily. Staff being transferred must be seen to be getting the best deal possible, and if you can offer staff the choice of whether to transfer or to be moved to different work that is remaining in-house, it may be an easier process to manage.

Avoiding conflict

The best way of averting difficulties is to ensure that everyone on your staff is fully aware of what is happening. Training schemes will explain what changes are taking place, and why. To do this is entirely in the spirit of many of the systems currently used by large organizations to demonstrate their management quality, such as the Investors in People standard or the Charter Mark. It could be a good idea to provide specific training on service level management for your staff, bringing together a cross-section of types and levels of seniority of staff where possible. Improved internal communications, maybe even an 'SLA newsletter' can help to explain changes, and to tell staff about amendments to the operation of the agreement. If those amendments are as a result of suggestions by specific staff members or teams, then make sure that the readers know this! In Chapter 12 we offer a number of ideas for improving the communication within the LIS itself and, of course, to the customers and the suppliers.

Improved communications with your supplier will also help everyone to cope. Are there regular meetings with the supplier to monitor progress? Perhaps staff members, separately from the negotiating team, can be observers at the meetings and take responsibility for telling their colleagues what happened there. A front-line staff member could speak up for the interests of library clients, and in doing so get to know the supplier's team better while the supplier meets the library's action team.

Business planning skills can be used to ensure that the problems are kept to a minimum. Proper project plans will highlight the critical dates when reports or meetings are due, and when information can be exchanged between the parties about how things are going. Staff can collect details of problems and successes to go on to the agenda of the regular checkpoint meetings. Staff may need to be trained for some of these roles, which again can be presented as a positive outcome from the changes.

Staff can be involved in marketing the new services and being spokesmen for the benefits of the changes. To do this they will need the sort of understanding that comes with being closely involved with the SLA development or operation process, which should lead to an understanding not only of where the difficulties lie but of some possible ways to resolve them.

Enlist your allies in the process of coping with your staff's natural disquiet at some of these changes. Keep the staff representatives (whether from a trades union or a staff association) involved in the changes, and attempt to deal openly and honestly with objections and fears. There may be a simple answer, or it may just be something that nobody has yet thought of, so consider each comment carefully. But you may need to be firm about the path that the library needs to follow, no matter how sympathetically you receive the representatives.

Above all, keep the channels of communication open and continuously engaged. Remember one final thing – management actions often speak louder than words. If you tell staff that all is well but act as if the library is under constant threat from an aggressive or predatory partner, they will act accordingly.

Management and reporting

When the LIS staff operating under an SLA remain members of the parent organization or manage staff members of the organization, there will need to be some written commitment to maintaining the staff management systems of the parent organization. Support staff expecting promotion or posting to another part of the company will expect not to be disadvantaged; similarly, librarians and information scientists intending to move to managerial posts, or to take up positions as information specialists within a production area of the company, expect that there will be a continuous record of their achievement. A contractor's staff may have to commit to learning the employing organization's staff appraisal system, and the company may have to re-examine its system to discover whether it can accommodate a situation in which contractors or consultants are present within the management line.

Opportunities for all

Sometimes there are opportunities to be able to show the staff that there is a very positive side to having an SLA, in that they may be able to acquire new skills in writing the SLA itself. It will also give staff and others the opportunity for self analysis and also to focus on being more accountable. Likewise, it will offer staff, perhaps for the first time, the opportunity to see the 'bigger picture' in how the LIS functions, relying upon, and linking together with other parts of the LIS and the organization and with the outside world. Other opportunities may occur in that staff can learn other new skills such as facilitator/teaching roles and not just act as a provider of information. There could be a shift in type of 'jobs' available, for example more roles in IT, project management and management of staff to undertake.

The LIS manager will need to be constantly aware of the opportunities to 'sell' the SLA to staff so that they take up a positive view of why and how it will affect the LIS.

Summary

In this chapter, we have seen that staff have legitimate concerns about what happens to them when service level management is introduced, and that it is often the front-line staff who have to take action to resolve difficulties between library, customers and suppliers. It is possible for management to take some positive steps to deal with the situation:

- Do not tire of explaining what is happening, and of putting fears to rest.
- Use as many channels of communication as you can think of.
- Be open with staff and show them what is going on.
- Be true to your words in your own relationships with staff, suppliers and customers.

12

COMMUNICATION STRATEGIES

In this chapter you will find out:

- why communication strategies are important
- different types of vehicles and other ideas to use in communicating
- things to watch to avoid conflict.

Why communication strategies are important

A frequently encountered problem with the introduction of service level agreements is the failure by one or more of the parties to understand what is involved. There is a failure of the communication that is essential if the parties are to reach the agreed statement of levels of service that is so necessary for success. So it is important that you give some thought to creating a communication strategy as part of your plans to introduce service level management.

Take the opportunities afforded by discussing the SLA with your customers to find out if other services are needed. It could be the right time to offer training, especially if a new service, for example new computerized services or subscriptions to electronically held journals, are being introduced. Ensure that everyone approaches the introduction of the SLA with the right attitude, promoting any changes as something positive, not just to do with budgets and cuts.

Exploit the strategic advantage you have of being the person who can say 'no' at any time: this could be in the situation where the LIS is not in a position to offer a service or buy a piece of information – perhaps an expensive journal or report that will have limited use for the rest of the organization and the customers. At the same time learn how and when you should make concessions in order to gain your objectives when negotiating the SLA. Also learn how to avoid being intimidated by users, suppliers or technical people. Get them to speak in plain language, thus avoiding any misunderstandings.

Service level agreements can seem threatening to many of those involved. In Chapter 11 we discussed the effects on managing staff, but it can also appear to your customers that you are becoming less approachable and somehow stepping aside from the organization. One means of improving people's acceptance of the new ways of organization, and their understanding, is to use the various channels of communication available to you in order to explain what is taking place.

Communication tools

You can use some or all of these tools.

Publications

Articles in the corporate newspaper or staff magazine can help to show the benefits of service level management, both for the customer in terms of knowing what to expect, and for the information centre, in terms of being able to plan better for future demand.

We saw in Chapter 11 that sometimes it may be more appropriate to have a special SLA newsletter, keeping people informed about the various aspects of the agreement and its development. It can be a useful vehicle to let users and staff know each of the steps being taken, and what can or cannot be expected of the various services provided by the LIS. The SLA newsletter could also be used as timely reminders of what the users are expected to do and provide.

A brochure could also be produced explaining the main elements of the

SLA, and might also include an invitation to the LIS to see the various services on offer.

Intranet

Use your organization's intranet to issue information about the way in which SLAs are being introduced and managed. The intranet has the advantage of being quick to update and, if you have suitable editorial software (such as FrontPage or HotMetal), you can rapidly produce pages to deal with any problems that arise.

Information pages such as these do not have to be the last word in web graphics and sophistication: if you have a standard template, or if the site is database driven, it is only a matter of typing in a short page of information.

Presentations

Take the time to invite your major users to a presentation about managing the library and information centre under service level agreements, and show them that although there will inevitably be changes, much will be as it was before. In particular, just because SLAs have been introduced, it will make no difference to the fact that the library is the primary source of expertise on a wide range of research topics, and on publications procurement. Presentations for your staff will also help to smooth the way. Explanations by the management of the information service will do more to improve staff relations than relying on the official notices put out by the organization's senior management.

Remember that those staff members doing the presenting need to have their presentational skills honed, so as to be seen by the users to be representative of a professionally competent service.

Personal contact

Because the LIS staff are in constant touch with the users it will be essential to ensure that all the staff are fully familiar with the content of the SLA and that they take every opportunity to explain the content as it affects a particular service under discussion. Staff should know what to tell, how to listen and how to explain, in jargon-free language, what services are on offer and at what price. So staff should be able to communicate effectively face to face, on the telephone and via mail or e-mail. Interpersonal communication skills, the ability to work with a wide variety of people successfully, are the number one reason why some people succeed and others fail. Also, listening is much more than just hearing – so learn how to really listen to the customers. Remember that people are very short of time and long, unstructured monologues are not conducive to the main message – that the LIS is offering a professional, business-like service.

Regular meetings

These should be an essential feature in the setting up and continuous monitoring of the SLA. Do not think that it is a waste of time arranging meetings, even with only a few people. The objective is to get the SLA right and ensure that everyone understands the elements of it. Regular face-to-face contact, for even a short meeting, will enable you to quickly get over any point that might not be clearly understood by your customers.

Training sessions

Presentations about service levels need not stand alone: that has the risk of making the introduction of SLAs seem even more forbidding. If they are covered as part of a wider training session, perhaps on improving services or getting best value from resources, then there is a greater chance of getting staff and others to understand and accept the changes.

Likewise always ensure that the LIS takes part in any induction courses that the organization may offer to newcomers. This way the LIS can be sure that everyone understands the agreements, while at the same time using the induction training opportunity to ensure that all services are known to the newcomers.

Open days

These offer opportunities to be able to 'sell' the services and at the same time introduce the SLA to users. Hosting open days – or even a series of such days in order to catch everyone – may also attract the missing 'non-users' of the LIS so that you are able to introduce the services, and the SLA itself.

Look for every opportunity to explain or promote the SLA.

Communication techniques

By now it must look as if the SLA brings with it the need to start using a whole range of communications techniques – although you may well realize that you have been using a number of them already. But consider this: the SLA itself is a communications tool. It sets out and communicates to others the service that the library (and its suppliers) offer, and may draw attention to elements of that service that users have not so far thought about. Maybe they do not use the 'alerting service' for example, and explaining what that is, and the standards applied, could be just what is needed to better communicate the library's strengths to the customers. Once the SLA is in place, it acts as a ready reference to tell everyone what the library does and to what standards. The SLA can, in the right hands, be a constantly visible advertisement for the library and information service!

Avoiding conflicts

Dealing with problems and avoiding conflicts must also be seen as a role of communications, and of course this is also one of the key functions of the SLA. But this aim will not be achieved without good communication between the parties to the agreement, both when negotiating it in the first place and when running it once it is in place and working. Be honest about what is up for discussion with both your customers and your suppliers.

Apart from the internal communications methods discussed above, you may need to set up further means of communication with the supplier and other interested parties. These could include regular scheduled meetings, reports at agreed intervals, or one-to-one discussions between library and company directors. Such meetings and reports need to be frank and open, so that if there is a problem the parties have the chance to resolve it before it becomes a crisis.

Summary

While library and information services frequently take great pains over their publicity activities, they are often not as dedicated to the idea of communication. The change demanded by service level management requires you to use every appropriate means of communication to explain to your customers what is happening:

- Emphasize what is remaining the same as well as what is changing. One of the main things that will be no different is your commitment to excellent service by the most appropriate means, and this is a powerful message for your communications.
- Involve any or all of your partners as you need. They will generally be pleased to make their people well known within their customer organizations.
- Look for every opportunity to explain what is going on, and consider creating new channels of communication if that is required.

Appendix 1

REFERENCES AND FURTHER READING

We have listed the references to text quoted in the various chapters and also added other references for those with further curiosity!

Chapter 1: The origins and use of service level agreements

1   [Course advertisement], Quadrilect, 1996.
2   Hiles, A. N., 'Service level agreements – panacea or pain?', *The TQM Magazine*, **6** (2), 1994, 14–16.
3   HM Treasury, Central Unit on Purchasing, *Service level agreements;* CUP Guidance 44, HM Treasury, 1994 (out of print).
4   Local Government, Planning and Land Act 1980, HMSO, 1980.
5   Local Government Act 1988, HMSO, 1988.
6   Department of the Environment, Transport and the Regions, *Modern local government: in touch with the people*, DETR, 1998, available at **www.local-regions.detr.gov.uk/lgwp/index.htm**
7   Department of National Heritage, *Reading the future: a review of public libraries in England*, Department of National Heritage, 1997.
8   Department of Health and Social Security, *Enquiry into National Health Service management*, DHSS, 1983.
9   Department of Health, *Working for Patients*, (Cm 555), HMSO, 1989.
10 Stewart, J. and Walsh, K., 'Change in the management of public services', *Public Administration*, **70** (4), (Winter 1992), 479–518. A useful source of detail for each of these initiatives.

11   Rayner Scrutinies, named after the Marks & Spencer managing direc-
      tor Sir Derek (now Lord) Rayner, were a series of departmental enquiries
      which took place in the early 1980s. With guidance from Sir Derek, who
      was based in the Cabinet Office, they aimed to identify ways in which
      departmental activities could be carried out more efficiently, and some
      early reviews of government libraries took place under these scrutinies.

12   House of Commons, Committee of Public Accounts,13th report,
      Financial Management Initiative (HC 61, 1986–87), HMSO, 1987.

13   Efficiency Unit, *Improving management in government: the next steps*,
      HMSO, 1988.

14   Ryan, C., 'Next Steps backwards', *Public Finance*, (12–18 January 2001),
      26–7.

15   HM Treasury, *Competing for quality* (Cm 1730), HMSO, 1991.

16   Bartlett, N., 'Service level agreements in Thames valley', *Police*, **25** (6),
      (February 1993), 16–17.

17   Home Office, Prison Service, *Prison libraries: roles and responsibilities*,
      [Prison service], 1992. Subsumed in Home Office, Prison Service,
      Prison libraries, Prison Service order 6710, Prison Service, 2000, avail-
      able at
      www.hmprisonservice.gov.uk/filestore/256_275.pdf
      Sample SLA is included at 32–3 of the later document.

18   Naylor, C., 'When the supplier selects', *Bookseller*, (18 February 2000),
      28–9; and 'Liverpool scores with supplier selection', *Bookseller*, (2 June
      2000), 28–9.

19   Available at
      www.cip.org.uk/cip/index.htm

20   Street, M., 'ISPs duck SLA obligations', *IT Week*, **4** (5), (5 February 2001),
      39. See also
      www.iowatch.com
      for details of the ISP performance surveys, and an example of moni-
      toring software.

21   Heery, M., 'Why an SLA will get in the way', *Library Manager*, (8),
      (June 1995), 10–12. Contains a list of such arguments against SLAs.

Further reading

Audit Commission, *Realising the benefits of competition: the client role for contract-ed services*, The Stationery Office, 1993.

Audit Commission, *Behind closed doors: the revolution of central support services*, The Stationery Office, 1994.

Blunt, P., 'Prison Library services: the prison library perspective', *Public Library Journal*, **9** (6), (Nov/Dec 1994), 163–5. Discusses the successful implementation of SLAs for library provision to prisons.

Burch, M., 'Service Level Agreements: are they worth it?'. In Knowles, B. (ed.), *Routes to quality: proceedings of the conference held at Bournemouth University, (29–31 August 1995)*, Buopolis 1, Bournemouth University Library and Information Services, 1996.

Capital Planning, *Sheffield and North Trent College of Nursing and Midwifery: provision of services under contract*, Capital Planning Information, 1991. A project to develop contract arrangements and a SLA to provide, with other libraries, services for the college.

Cartwright, D., 'SLAve to smallprint', *Information Week*, 62, (7 April 1999), 33–4.

Chivers, B. and Thebridge, S., 'Best value in public libraries: the role of research'. In *Library Management*, **21** (9), 2000, 456–65.

Corrall, S.M., 'The access model, managing the transformations at Aston University', *Interlending and Document Supply*, **21** (4), 1993, 13–23. Aston University Library and Information Services has followed an 'access' strategy since 1985–86, adopting the model of a specialized industrial information service. Its style of provision is characterized by services tailored to customer needs, innovation through IT and devolved financial management. Service level agreements for 'standard' and 'tailored' services are being developed with academic departments in the context of a trading company model.

Favret, L., 'Benchmarking, annual library plans and Best Value: the implications for public libraries', *Library Management*, **21** (7), 2000, 340–8.

Foster, A., 'Convincing others of the need for change', *Library Manager*, **2**, (Dec. 1994), 20–1. Describes the development of a total information strategy.

Considers the use of SLAs as a means of achieving targets for service provision.

Library Association, *A charter for public libraries*, Library Association, 1993.

Liddle, D., 'Best Value – the impact on libraries: practical steps in demonstrating Best Value', *Library Management*, **20** (4), [1999], 206–14.

Powell, A., 'Management modes and measurement in a virtual library', *Special Libraries*, **85** (4), (Fall 94), 260–3. Discusses SLAs and the approach developed by Robert Kaplan of Harvard University called a 'balanced score card'.

Revill, D. and Ford, G. (eds.), *Working papers on Service Levels Agreements*, SCONUL, 1994. Macartney, N. [Reviews], *Journal of Documentation*, **51** (4), 1995, 423–5.

Chapter 2: What is a service level agreement?

1   Robinson, G. and Bakewell, K., 'Say what you mean: the British Standard glossary of documentation terms', *Information and Library Manager*, **9** (3), 1990, 13–15.

2   Audit Commission, *Behind closed doors: the revolution in central support services*, HMSO, 1994.

Further reading

Smith, R., 'Business continuity planning and SLAs', *Information Management and Computer Security*, **3** (3), 1995, 17–19. Business continuity planning justifies an SLA; establishment and maintenance of SLAs.

Chapter 3: Who the agreement is between and the other items you need to put into the SLA

1   Library Association, *Code of professional conduct and guidance notes*, 3rd edn, Library Association, 1999 (under revision, 2001).

2   Cabinet Office, *Service first: the new charter programme*, Cabinet Office, 1998.

Chapter 4: What the SLA document should look like and descriptions of services

1   Library Association, *Model statement of standards for public library services*, Library Association, 1995.

2   Department of National Heritage, *Reading the future: a review of public libraries in England*, Department of National Heritage, 1997.

3   Investors in People UK, *The Investors in People standard*, Investors in People, 1996.

4   Library Association, *Framework for continuing professional development*, Library Association, [1992], reprinted and updated at intervals.

5   The ISM is now available only as a CD-ROM (although earlier versions were paper bound); the current edition is available from the British Computer Society.

Further reading

KPMG UK, *Service level agreements methodology*, KPMG UK, 1998.
Private Finance Panel, *Basic contractual terms*, Private Finance Panel, 1996.
Private Finance Panel, *Writing an output specification*, Private Finance Panel, 1996.

Chapter 5: Service monitoring

1   Department of National Heritage, *Reading the future: a review of public libraries in England*, Department of National Heritage, 1997, 34.

2   Brandt, W. D., 'The intelligence bottleneck: too much supply – too little demand', *Journal of the Association for Global Strategic Information*, 2 (2), (July 1993), 86–99. Cited in Clark, P. E., 'Client aspirations and relationships: issues for the information manager'. In *New roles, new skills, new people*, University of Hertfordshire Press, 1995. Discussions of the difficulties of establishing suitable performance management systems for information services within the accounting regimes of many organizations.

3   Reuters Business Information, *Information as an asset: the invisible goldmine*,

Reuters Business Information, 1995.

4   The European Council of Information Associations, *Euroguide LIS – the guide to competencies for the European professional in Library and Information Services*, Aslib, the Association for Information Management, 1999.

5   Audit Commission, *Realising the benefits of competition: the client rôle for contracted services*, HMSO, 1993.

Further reading

Flynn, R. and Williams, G. (eds), *Contracting for health*, OUP, 1997. The following are among the chapters:

• Hughes, D., McHale, J. V. and Griffiths, L., 'Settling contract disputes in the National Health Service: formal and informal pathways'.

• Lapsley, I. and Llewellyn, S., 'Statements of mutual faith: soft contracts in social care'.

Maddock, S. and Morgan, G., 'Barriers to transformation: beyond bureaucracy and the market conditions for collaboration in health and social care', *International Journal of Public Service Management*, **11** (4), 1998, 234–51. The effects of change in relationships in the NHS.

Sale, M., 'In Memoriam: performance indicators and time analysis in the Bibliographic Records Section of Aston University Library and Information Services', *Library Review*, **45** (2), 1996, 58–65. Shows performance indicators . . . in light of the development of an SLA.

Chapter 6: Charging for services

1   Armstrong, A., 'Analysing industrial information service costs: a simple check list', *Aslib Proceedings*, **24** (11), 1972. Reprinted in Roberts, S. A. (ed.), *Costing and economics of library and information services*, Aslib reader series 5, Aslib, 1984. Despite its age, the list of elements contained in this paper is comprehensive and only needs updating by the addition of the cost of electronic services that have become commonplace in LIS

since it was written. A highly detailed model is developed in Roberts, S. A., *Cost management for library and information services*, Butterworth, 1985.

2   Woodsworth, A. and Williams, J. F., *Managing the economics of owning, leasing and contracting out information services*, Ashgate, 1993. Chapter 7, 'Costs and charging strategies', examines each option in detail, although the approach is North American.

Further reading

Bates, M. E., 'Fee-based information services within special libraries', *Library Management Briefings*, (Spring 1998), 1–7.

Foster, A., 'Time to rethink charging strategies', *Library Manager*, (6), (April 1995), 15. Various reasons advanced for charging for services in a library suggest that academic libraries might consider the use of SLAs for interdepartmental charges.

Synder, H. and Davenport, E., *Costing and pricing in the digital age*, Library Association Publishing, 1997.

Chapter 7: Managing your customers

1   CPI Ltd, *Consulting the customer: using market research in libraries: proceedings of a seminar held in October 1998*, CPI Ltd, 1999.

2   Kerr, G., *Gaining and Retaining Customer Loyalty*, Occasional Paper 3, CPI Ltd, 1999.

Further reading

Hiles, A. N., *Service level agreements*, Chapman and Hall, 1993. Describes how to manage the service relationship between provider and customer. Defines the level of service that a customer can expect. It is appropriate to all in-house services where legal contracts do not exist.

Chapter 8: Outsourcing services

1   Burge, S., *Much pain, little gain: privatisation and UK government libraries*, IFLA, 64th conference, August 1998, Amsterdam, [proceedings], available at
    www.ifla.org
2   Quoted in 'Enhancing governmental productivity through competition: a new way of doing business within the government, to provide quality government at least cost: a progress report on OMB, Circular No. A-76, "performance of commercial activities"', [Washington, D.C.], Office of Management and Budget, Office of Federal Procurement Policy, 1988.
3   White, H S., Library oursourcing and contracting: cost-effectiveness or shell game?, In *Librarianship – quo vadis?*, USA, Libraries Unlimited, 2000, 297–7.
4   Dunk, L., *Outsourcing and externalisation by libraries, museums and archives: literature review*, [London, CPI for Resource], 2000.
5   Helen Kist, managing director of Iowatch, quoted in *IT week*, 5 February 2001, 39.

Further reading

Adam, R., 'The invisible market', *Bookseller*, (6 October 2000), 38–40. Reports the first survey into the library market for bibliographic data.

Bates, M. E., 'Catalog outsourcing: no clear-cut choice. Outsourcing library technical operation; practices in academic, public and special libraries', *Information Outlook*, **1** (4), (April 1997), 21–4 .

Bates, M. E., 'Avoiding the ax: how to keep from being downsized or outsourced', *Information Outlook*, (October 1997), 18–21.

Bates, M. E., 'Emerging trends in information brokering', *Competitive Intelligence Review*, (Winter 1997), 48–53.

Bates, M. E., 'Outsourcing, co-sourcing, and core competencies: what's an information professional to do?', *Information Outlook*, (December 1999), 35–7.

Broadbent, J. and Laughlin, R., 'Contractual changes in schools and general practices: professional resistance and the role of absorption and absorbing groups'. In Flynn, R. and Williams, G. (eds), *Contracting for health: quasi-markets and the National Health Service*, OUP, 1997, 30–46.

CPI Ltd, *The concept of best value: the impact on library services. Proceedings of a seminar held in September 1998,* CPI Ltd., 1998. A major report on supplier selection of library stock in public libraries, published by CPI as Library and Information Commission Report No. 20. The project reported on was carried out for the British National Bibliography Research Fund with the collaboration of Westminster City Council and Hertfordshire Libraries. The report describes and evaluates the pilot projects undertaken by the two library authorities and provides some key advice on the practicalities from both the library and suppliers' point of view.

CPI Ltd, *Best value and libraries: the reality beckons? Proceedings of a seminar held in September 1999,* CPI Ltd, 1999.

CPI Ltd, *Library purchasing consortia in the UK: activity benefits and practice*, CPI Ltd, 1999. This major 180-page report, published by CPI on behalf of LIC as Library and Information Commission Report No. 16, is based on research undertaken by Jo Pye and David Ball, of Bournemouth University. The report provides an important, analytical review of how purchasing consortia operate across the various library sectors – public, higher education, further education, health.

CPI Ltd, *Outsourcing book selection: supplier selection in public libraries*, Library and Information Commission Research Report 20, CPI Ltd, 1999 (executive summary available at **www.lic.gov.uk/publications/executivesumaries/index.html.**

Dunk, L., *Outsourcing and externalisation by libraries, museums and archives: literature review*, Resource Research Project LIC/RE/108, June 2000. Linda Dunk, Research Assistant, Bournemouth, UK, compiled this review, which has an extensive bibliography.

Edmonds, D., 'Facilities management for information services: outsourcing the impossible', *Serials*, **11** (1), (November 1998), 219–22.

Liddle, D., *Best value – are libraries leading or following?*, Occasional Paper 1, CPI Ltd, 1999.

Streatfield, D. et al., *Best value and better performance in libraries*, Library and Information Commission Research Report 52, Information Management Associates, 1999, brief abstract available at **www.lic.gov.uk/publications/index.html**

Chapter 9: Managing your suppliers

Further reading

Ball, D. and Pye, J., 'Library purchasing consortia in the UK: activity and practice', *Library and Information Briefings*, **88**, 1999, 1–15.

'Building relationships with suppliers' (themed issue), *The TQM Magazine*, **5** (5), (October 1993).

CPI Ltd, *Changing relationships: new dimensions in library supply: proceedings of a seminar held in December 1998,* CPI Ltd, 1998.

Eden, R., 'Bookfund tendering, assessment and evaluation – the librarian's viewpoint', *Taking Stock*, 1998, 7–11.

Gambles, B., 'Procurement: new skills for best value?', *Library and Information Appointments*, **3** (17), (11 August 2000), App. 373–4.

Greenhalgh, N., *Managing supplier relationships*, HMSO, 1993.

Hardwood, P. and Prior, A., 'The role and service of subscription agents', *Library and Information Briefings*, 81, 1998, 2–12.

Lancaster, N., 'Bookfund tendering, assessment and evaluation – the supplier's viewpoint', *Taking Stock*, 1998, 1–6.

Naylor, C., 'When the supplier selects', *Bookseller*, (18 February 2000), 28–9.

Naylor, C., 'Liverpool scores with supplier selection', *Bookseller*, (2 June 2000), 28–9.

Pye, J. and Ball, D., *Library purchasing consortia in the UK: activity benefits and practice*, CPI Ltd., 1999.

Sidebottom, D., 'Tendering for library services and supplies', *Serials*, **11** (3), (November 1998), 224–5.

Wootton, D., 'Managing your service suppliers', *Managing Information*, **6** (4), (May 1999), 41–3.

Chapter 10: Managing your e-suppliers

Further reading

Bates, M. E., 'How to implement electronic subscriptions: replacing the routing list hassle', *Online*, (May 1998), 80–6.

Lister Cheese, A., *Electronic information resources from Swets Blackwell. Proceedings of 'e-OSHE World: Seeing the Future' Conference, Dublin, Ireland, Friday 23 June 2000,* available at
http://panizzi.shef.ac.uk/EOSHE
e-mail: Alistercheese@uk.swetsblackwell.com

Percy, R., 'Library services: managing successful outsourcing in the digital age'. In *Digital library technology 97: transforming library services for the digital age – meeting user needs for electronic information delivery: proceedings of IES Conference, Chatswood, NSW, Australia*, IES Conferences, 1997.

Chapter 11: Managing staff

Further reading

Goulding, A. et al., *Likely to succeed: attitudes and aptitudes for an effective information profession in the 21st century*, Library and Information Commission Research Report 8, available at
www.lic.gov.uk/publications/index.html

TFPL Ltd, *Skills for knowledge management: a briefing paper, based on research undertaken by TFPL on behalf of The Library and Information Commission*, LIC, June 1999 (executive summary and also full text available at
www.lic.gov.uk/publications/index.html).

Chapter 12: Communication strategies

Further reading

Leigh, A. and Maynard, M., *Perfect communications: all you need to get it right first time*, Random House, 1993.

Contact addresses

CPI reports are available from:

CPI Ltd, 91 High Street, Bruton, Somerset BA10 0BH, UK

Tel: +44 (0) 17 4981 2963 Fax: +44 (0) 17 4981 2964

e-mail: enquiries@cpi-ltd.com

IMA reports are available from:

Information Management Associates, 28 Albion Road, Twickenham
    TW2 6QZ, UK

Tel: +44 (0) 20 8755 0471 Fax: +44 (0) 20 8755 0471

e-mail: streatfield@compuserve.com

Appendix 2

SAMPLE QUARTERLY REPORT FORMAT

General purpose report

SERVICE LEVEL AGREEMENT XYZ Co LIS

Quarterly report to Widget Sales Team (WST)

Date and tax point 1 December 2000

Item	Number	Tariff charge (£)	Total (£)
Enquiries	107	10.00	1,070.00
Publications indexed	726	3.27	2,374.02
Loans	136	2.70	367.20
Photocopies	1426*	5.80	8,270.80
Training	4.5 (hours)	115.00/hour	517.50
TOTAL			12,599.52
VAT on items marked *		1,447.40	14,046.92

VAT levied at standard rate of 17.5%

VAT registration number 00 0000 000

Payment by credit transfer through Finance Department is due within 6 weeks

Profiled spend to date: 73.5%

Actual spend to date: 69.3%

Projected out-turn: 99.8%

Highlights

Subscriptions for all 23 journals for WST were renewed before the target date of 30 November 2000 and continuous delivery for 2001 is assured.

Enquiries continued above the notional target level of 100 per month for the third month in succession. WST is likely to overshoot its target level by 13% by the end of the financial year and may incur additional charges to represent the transfer of resources from other projects.

Negotiation of targets for 2002–3 should begin in January 2002, with the aim of completion by 16 February 2002. The level of enquiries will need to be examined at this point.

BLDSC continues to supply photocopies within the target times and the 1426 units billed this month include 23 urgent requests for which multiple units are charged.

Fourteen photocopies were requested from *Marketing Week* and the LIS recommends that this title should be added to the journals list supplied to WST, as this would result in a reduction of overall costs.

Publication ordered but outstanding for more than 8 weeks:
Smith, J. and Jones, S., *Modern widget design*, Technical Press, 1998.

Publication cancelled and reordered from another supplier after 13 weeks on order:
A widget on every billhook, Business Publishing House, 1997.

Custom elements

Further elements that may be required are the following:

* training given (induction, board presentations, etc.)

- file sections checked (for an SLA including records management)
- methods of checking and levels of sampling
- number of files handled during reporting period
- statement of problems encountered and remedies applied.

Service failure reports

A number of elements typically found in computer SLAs may be useful here. Usually, definitions are set for various levels of service failure.

Appendix 3

OTHER POSSIBLE LIS FUNCTIONS TO ADD TO AN SLA

There will inevitably be a number of miscellaneous functions that the LIS carries out for the client organization. The following list suggests some of those that may exist in your LIS, or that may be considered appropriate to include in an SLA.

The principle of change control means that none of these is permanently excluded if not listed in the initial agreement, but it may be good policy to include authority to continue these activities in the initial agreement to avoid needing to invoke change control at a later date. A service specification prepared by a non-LIS management team is likely to exclude many of these services. Therefore, if you are using this book to help to prepare a bid against a tender document, it would be useful to include services such as these as an additional item. A simple statement along the following lines should precede the list:

> **XYZ LIS will also provide the following services not listed in the service specification, in order to continue existing LIS good practice and co-operative arrangements. The cost of these services is included in the total costs indicated.**

The Audit Commission and others suggest that, as experience builds up between the parties and trust grows, the number of items included in an SLA will shorten and exhaustive lists should be avoided. This may be better advice in simpler areas such as tendering for local authority manual services, but the approach that we suggest here fits comfortably with that view if one or two of our preferred strategies are adopted. The Audit Commission does concede that the contracts for white-collar services such as legal or architectural services are likely to be more complex.

First, these additional services should appear in a service marketing brochure, which forms an annexe to the main agreement, which, in turn, should refer to there being a current edition of this services brochure. This allows new services to be included or superseded services to be withdrawn by mutual agreement or by LIS management as part of its normal work without the need continually to invoke change control. Second, a selection should be made from these suggestions to ensure that the agreement includes the most important services that your LIS at present provides. For the remainder, a phrase such as 'other services provided by arrangement or agreement' will allow you to offer further services from the list that are not among your LIS's present operations but may become important during the lifetime of the agreement. This catch-all wording lets you offer these extra or enhanced services whenever required without the need for formal change control.

The list of services might include items from the following:

- maintaining exchange agreements, including those on listing, indexing, cataloguing and processing stock
- keeping XYZ staff up to date regarding new acquisitions
- collecting official or commercial information produced within [country] on [agreed subjects]
- collecting statistics of LIS use (and possibly publishing the results annually)
- ensuring that publications are supplied to members of courses mounted by XYZ training staff
- ensuring that the necessary films, videos, and slides are available for training programmes
- giving lectures on the importance and availability of information either to training courses or as part of induction courses.

Establishing an exchange of information agreement with other organizations

This will probably need some impetus from a high level to ensure an integrated, co-ordinated approach. It may also be necessary to set this in an agreement because the LIS's approach to competitor organizations may be different from that found in other parts of the organization.

Establishing international connections for the purpose of exchanging information

This will involve keeping up to date with developments in IT and, as appropriate, making proposals to introduce them into your LIS. There may be wider implications within the organization's office technology policy. The inclusion of this target will give the LIS an official remit to propose such changes, which, given the specialist nature of many LIS-specific software, may not fit smoothly with wider organizational IT standards.

Liaison with publications unit press office or publicity unit

The creation and maintenance of databases [such as]:

- references to information held at XYZ Co.
- of ongoing projects and research including collections of 'grey literature'
- of organizations, consultants and specialists in [named subject fields]
- of organizations with whom the Information Section has established exchange agreements
- collections of internal reports written by XYZ Co. staff.

Responsibility for an exhibition area in the XYZ Co. buildings [showing documents produced by XYZ Co., themed around the organization's activities, or providing a general showcase for the LIS].

Provision of translation and linguistics services [either in-house or by establishing contracts with external translation services].

Managing donations and free subscriptions – renewals, receipts, circulation and filing.

Operation of a public enquiries service, to receive and answer a wide range of enquiries from the UK and beyond. [It is useful to obtain the organization's agreement to any form of service to the public, and, if relevant, to establish the level of service (e.g. to postgraduate researchers only).]

Monitor and report on the effectiveness of the XYZ Co. LIS.

Prepare and agree an annual programme of work within the organization's accounting and budgeting system. [This should include forward look which will set the environment for future years' work and budget bids.]

Train XYZ Co. staff in the most cost-effective use of the LIS, including the use of IT services (CD-ROM, internet, etc.).

Maintain a guide to information services, listing the available services, contact addresses and telephone and fax numbers [to ensure that XYZ Co. staff are kept aware of the services available].

Maintain services on the company's Intranet, including publication of the library catalogue, contact databases and databases of company expertise [etc.].

Many organizations include records management within their LIS, in which case a number of appropriate clauses need to be added to reflect this additional area of work. Standards are often set by an SLA, for example, the average or maximum retrieval and delivery times for documents or files recalled from store.

In an SLA for an LIS it may be sufficient to refer to another document setting out the agreement for records services, or a full agreement for records may be included in the current SLA. Referring to a separate document may be useful if it allows change control for either records or for the LIS to take place without the need to involve in the negotiations people who are unrelated to the function.

Representational duties

XYZ Co. LIS will represent the interests of XYZ Co. and attend professional meetings, provide advice and guidance on its behalf as appropriate.

Standard of advice, guidance and professional work

XYZ LIS is required to provide services of a high standard in its areas of activity, and will ensure that all information acquired is indexed and maintained professionally, ready for use by staff and others. This will include the maintenance of the databases, etc.

Involvement in training

XYZ Co. LIS staff will be involved in any training courses designated to demonstrate good practices and it will be ensured that staff are trained in the efficient use of databases, CD-ROMs, etc. and the internet.

XYZ LIS will invest in the highest possible standard of staff training to ensure that the quality and range of services offered to customers are constantly of the standard required. This is particularly necessary in the fast-changing area of computerized information services.

The XYZ Co. LIS manager will ensure that regular reminders are issued to staff about the procedures laid down by XYZ Co. senior management for dealing with public enquiries. These notices will include the requirements of open government, data protection, Charter Mark and other legislation or initiatives and may be issued in printed or electronic form as appropriate.

XYZ LIS will revise, revamp and extend the choice of services and options to meet the changing needs of all its customers, from internal users in the UK to the varying levels of public enquirers.

The LIS will ensure that financial and accounting controls are in place that fulfil the requirements of XYZ Co. [and its auditors].

Service standards

The service standards that have been included within this document are indicative only. The supplier will assess current performance during the initial six-month period of this Agreement. The information generated during that period will be used as a basis for the supplier and client to agree on the performance targets to be set for the remainder of the period of this Agreement.

It shall be the aim of the supplier to achieve continuing improvement in performance during the period of the Agreement. Performance targets will be appraised annually in the light of actual performance during previous periods, taking account of any special factors that may have, or will, apply.

While certain standards relating to specific areas of service have been specified above, it is expected that the supplier will achieve these levels of service standards throughout all operations and not just in those areas specifically monitored. The supplier will only be held responsible for performance during the period of this Agreement. Should errors that were made previous to 31 March 2001 be identified, they will be discounted for the purposes of assessing supplier performance.

It is recognized that pressing demands elsewhere may result in the supplier being required to release key staff, either temporarily or permanently. Should the extent of such requirements be significant, there may be a need to re-examine the requisite standards of service delivery in the affected areas.

In addition to producing the above information the supplier will, during the 2001–2 financial year, conduct a customer survey to gauge the extent of customer satisfaction with the service being provided. The form of this survey will be subject to agreement between both parties. In this survey, the supplier is expected to achieve a minimum of 95% of customers indicating overall service satisfaction.

In addition to the quarterly report, the supplier shall prepare annually and present a comprehensive report on its activities for each financial year. This report will show full year performance against each of the performance indicators and will, in addition, detail out-turn financial performance and performance in any policy areas of activity. This report shall be presented within three months of the end of the financial year. The annual report shall inform negotiations between client and supplier on targets (financial and other) for the revised SLA.

It is recognized by both parties that the reporting carried out in connection with this Agreement should, as far as is reasonably practicable, form an integral part of XYZ Co.'s overall reporting procedures. If required, amendments to the form and timing of these reports will be made in order to achieve that objective. It is also recognized that the information-gathering procedures and facilities are unlikely to be in place during the initial period of this Agreement. Consequently, there will be no requirement on the supplier to produce the stipulated quarterly reports during the initial six-month period of the Agreement, although a report for the initial six-month period shall be presented within three months of the end of the financial year.

Appendix 4

LIST OF DEFINITIONS

The following definitions may assist in compiling your own SLA; refer particularly to Chapters 3 and 4. Other definitions will be needed as you develop your agreement.

Abstracting   Making and recording on the LIS database a summary of the information in a document that has been catalogued and/or indexed there.

Additional LIS   Services in addition to those listed at paragraph 0.0 [in the SLA]: these are enumerated and described in an annexe to the SLA agreement.

Advisory services   Advice to sections on the indexing of publications, and the organization and classification of collections of publications or of other information resources held within the sections of XYZ Co.

Best value   'The duty of Best Value is one that local authorities will owe to local people, both as taxpayers and the customers of local authority services. Performance plans should support the process of local accountability to the electorate. Achieving Best Value is not just about economy and efficiency, but also about effectiveness and the quality of local services – the setting of targets and performance against these should therefore underpin the new regime.' Department of the Environment, Transport and the Regions, press release, 'New duty of best value for local authority services', 15 September 1999.

Binding   Preparation of XYZ Co. sections' material for binding or rebinding by a chosen external contractor.

Budget   The sum of money provided by the organization for the operation of the LIS, probably expressed as an annual amount of money. It may
be subdivided, for example into bookfund, staff salaries budget, periodicals fund, electronic databases fund, and so on: and the amounts fixed may
include an element for value-added tax on certain purchases or for costs
associated with salaries such as earnings-related national insurance contributions (ERNICs).

Cataloguing   The creation of bibliographic records according to stated and
agreed standards and their incorporation into the LIS database.

Change control   A means of agreeing and recording changes to contracts
or SLAs using procedures specified in the agreement. It is likely to include
a statement showing whose agreement is required to any changes, how the
changes and the agreement to them are to be recorded, and whether
there is any time limit to those changes (i.e. whether they run for the
remainder of the agreement and become part of it for renewal, or whether
they take place for a fixed length of time). It is also likely to record the location of a master copy of the contract that is agreed by all parties to be the
definitive version.

Circulation of periodicals (circulation management)   The distribution
by company messengers of consecutive issues of periodicals to their users
throughout the company, passed on in sequence using a circulation list
based on customers' requests to receive copies on circulation. Certain periodicals may not be available on circulation or for use outside the LIS. When
using electronic journals, the circulation of either the title, table of contents and/or full text is simultaneous to all readers.

Compulsory competitive tendering (CCT)   Another form of market
testing used in the local government sector, involving an obligation to put
services out for tender by external suppliers against whom the authority's
staff team would compete in delivering efficient and cost-effective serv-
ice(s). Now superseded by Best Value initiative.

Company Alert   A current awareness service based on the regular production
and circulation of a list of recently acquired LIS materials likely to be of interest to customers (e.g. based on XYZ Co. interests, or reflecting the interests

of divisions in a given building). Company Alert will be published every Wednesday. Separate editions will be produced for the research laboratories LIS on the second and fourth Fridays of every month.

Copyright advice   Advice to company sections on aspects of copying from published sources. Administration of the photocopying licences to the XYZ Co. from the Copyright Licensing Agency, the Newspaper Licensing Agency and Ordnance Survey, and advice to sections on licensed copying.

e-delivery   Electronic delivery of documents, journals and other information. Could be delivered via the internet, websites, CD-ROM, DVD, or other electronic vehicles.

Disposal of publications   The disposal of materials no longer required by sections.

Document supply   The supply of photocopies of extracts from documents in LIS's stock, regulated by the provisions of the law of copyright, and the additional provisions of the licences from the Copyright Licensing Agency and the Newspaper Licensing Agency held by XYZ Co.

Alternatively, the supply of extracts from documents held in remote databases by commercial and other suppliers is regulated by agreements in force concerning the copyright in those documents.

Enquiry and reference services   Answering enquiries on all subjects of corporate interests based on a collection of publications held as reference material and/or for lending at the main LIS and branches, and using external sources to support these collections.

Externalization   Provision of all aspects of a current service through a company or trust established for the purpose.

Indexing   The creation or enhancement of bibliographic records with terms from the indexing language listed in [*Chemical Abstracts*] in order to allow their later retrieval for current awareness or in response to enquiries.

Information retrieval   The retrieval and presentation of selected records taken from remote computer-held databases, or from databases on CD-ROM held in the LIS. Unless otherwise specified in the annexe of the SLA, searches are carried out in the LIS, by LIS staff, using information provided by the customer.

Interlibrary loans   Loans of material borrowed from other LIS arranged through the XYZ Co. LIS for its customers.

Loan of LIS material   A service of lending documents from the LIS stock to customers in XYZ Co. for notified durations of time.

Market testing   Government initiative used to test effectiveness, efficiency and costing of service providers against external providers.

Outsourcing   Contracting all or part of the activities to an outside organization or individual.

Purchase of publications   The purchase and provision, for use within the XYZ Co., of documents specified by customers for purposes that make the provision of a loan copy or copies inappropriate, but subject to any restrictions on supply brought about by the LIS's budgetary management, and otherwise at the LIS's discretion.

Sale of sectional publications   Where specified in the annexe of the SLA, the sale of and accounting for publications by sections within XYZ Co.

Selective dissemination of information (SDI)   A service providing current information from the LIS, or from external databases, to selected customers or groups of customers in the company, by matching the indexing terms of newly published materials with the search profiles of customers.

Value-added tax (see also **Budget)**   Tax paid on some materials purchased by LIS. At the time of going to press this includes electronic information services, elements of some subscriptions, telephone services, photocopying and some printing but LIS managers should check the current position and take appropriate advice when drawing up an SLA.

INDEX